Arrival of the India Mail Boat, c. 1844.

[*Frontispiece*

FOLKESTONE
THE STORY OF A TOWN

BY

C. H. BISHOP

M.A. (Cantab), M.A. (London), Ph.D. (Nott'm)

HEADLEY BROTHERS LTD
THE INVICTA PRESS ASHFORD KENT

TO
FOLKESTONIANS
EVERYWHERE

First printed May, 1973
Reprinted January, 1974
Revised and reprinted, January, 1982

ISBN 0 900443 10 3

Printed in Great Britain by Headley Brothers Ltd The Invicta Press Ashford Kent and London

CONTENTS

ILLUSTRATIONS

Arrival of the India Mail Boat, *c.* 1844   *frontispiece*

FIGURES IN THE TEXT

iv

PREFACE

THE aim of this book is to give a general outline history of the town of Folkestone. No continuous history has so far been written, the nearest being S. J. Mackie's *Folkestone and its Neighbourhood* published with *Gleanings from the Municipal Records* in 1883. Much has happened since then and many of the records have since been lost; and the crowded events of the past century are already fading from human memory. Visitors and students frequently enquire about various aspects of the town's development, but no suitable modern book of reference has been available for many years. It is time one was written.

The task has not been easy. The evidence of the early period is very scanty, and the attempt to condense the events of so many years is liable to give a false impression. A detailed history would require many volumes. One can only try to give some idea of the way Folkestone people lived in years gone by and of the problems they faced. In an attempt to make the past live and to see things with their eyes we have freely quoted from contemporary sources and so tried to catch the spirit of the times.

It is with pleasure and gratitude that I acknowledge the help and encouragement of many friends and acquaintances, especially of Mr. J. F. Moncrieff, J.P.; I also wish to thank Mr. K. C. Sussams and Mr. C. P. Davies for their interest and advice; Miss J. M. Potter for material supplied for Chapter six, and Rev. A. H. Gibson for advice on Part I. To all these, to many of my friends, and to my wife who has shared my interest in Folkestone's history, I offer my sincere thanks.

Folkestone
December 1972

PART I

ANCIENT HISTORY

)

CHAPTER ONE

FOLKESTONE : THE BEGINNINGS

FOLKESTONE is known today chiefly as a delightful seaside resort and as a cross-channel port. With its spacious lawns, pleasant gardens and stately avenues it gives the impression of a distinctly modern town. Apart from the Parish Church all the houses and public buildings are of fairly recent origin and there is little to suggest that it was an ancient town. It has no castle, no cathedral, no ruins of ancient monasteries or colleges. Yet the town has an eventful history which stretches back as far as any in England.

But we do not know for certain when or how Folkestone came into existence, nor do we know how it got its name. We are obliged therefore to surmise from such evidence as we can find. The early historians tell us that it was originally a Saxon settlement, 'and most probably had its origin soon after the building of the castle and nunnery by King Eadbald, on the cliff close to the sea shore'. Under the protection of the castle, they say, a fishing village grew up. There, sheltered from the south-westerly gales by the projecting cliffs, fishermen could pull their boats up on the Stade at the mouth of the Pent stream. This is probably true of the Saxon settlement from which the present town had its origin.

A suspicion of earlier occupation was suggested by the fact that Roman tiles and coins had been found on the cliff top, and even walls containing fragments of 'Britaine brickes'. Camden, writing in 1610, suggested:

'Folkstone was a flourishing place in times past, as may appeere by the peeces of Romane coine and Britaine brickes daily there found: but under what name is uncertaine. Probable it is, that it was one of those towres or *holdes*, which in the reigne of Theodosius the younger (A.D. 346), the Romans placed to keep off the Saxons, as *Gildas* saith, at certaine distances along the shore in the south part of Britaine.'

Camden was recording an ancient tradition and connecting it with what he had read in older writers; but his surmise has

3

been shown to be partly correct by the excavations made in recent times in East Wear Bay. However there were earlier settlers in possession of the locality long before the Romans came, and some evidence of their occupation has been uncovered from time to time.

In recent years developments in Archaeology have revealed a little more of the history of pre-Saxon Kent, and we can say with some confidence that the place we call Folkestone must have been of some importance even in pre-Roman times. This was inevitable when we consider that east Kent was so close to the continent, and that the mouth of the Pent stream offered a convenient landing place for immigrant peoples. We have only to look at the map of Kent to see a number of ancient names which denote the regular landing places round the coast: Westgate, Margate, Ramsgate, and Sandgate. The suffix 'gate' meant a 'way' or 'road'; it is an ancient Norse word and still survives in the names of many streets in Britain, e.g. Burgate, Snargate, Broadgate. If we climb to the top of the Downs behind Folkestone we can clearly see some of these 'gates' up from the sea as depressions or clefts in the coast line. Now the Folkestone valley carved out by the Pent stream is one of these and it offered an easy way into the interior. An ancient name for this valley was probably 'Seagate' which was the name of one of the oldest streets in the town.

The valley led into the heart of the Folkestone plain, a broad wedge-shaped plateau between the hills and the sea; it was covered with trees and very fertile. It was very likely that some immigrants would settle at the mouth of the Pent stream, living by fishing along the shore and establishing small farms close inland. And so a fishing village would be established, these early settlers being perhaps, of Celtic origin.

THE CELTS

About 500 B.C. we know that groups of Celtic invaders came to occupy east Kent, and they were generally known as Britons. For several centuries before Caesar's first landing in 55 B.C., these bands of settlers had crossed the Channel or the North Sea to found homesteads in this island. They spoke different dialects of the Celtic group of languages, and they seem to have arrived here in three main waves, about 500 B.C., about 250 B.C. and again about 100 B.C. They were not members of a single nation, but they lived in small tribal units, each with its own 'rix' or chieftain, and they brought with them their iron weapons, their skill in crafts, their religion, their customs and their laws. They were, in fact, what the archaeologists call the Iron Age Folk, and the three groups we have mentioned above correspond to the archaeologists' divisions of British Iron Age A, B, and C.

The last tribes to cross into Kent soon after 100 B.C. were the Belgae who came from the lower Rhine; they were opposed by the earlier inhabitants, but eventually they dominated Kent south-east of the Medway. These were the peoples Caesar had to face when he made his first expedition into Britain, and very warlike was his reception. They had established a number of hill forts and cliff forts to which they repaired in times of danger, and from which the warriors emerged to attack the invader.

CLIFF FORTS

We get further information about these cliff forts from Caesar and Dio Cassius. When in 56 B.C. Caesar advanced north-westward into Gaul he encountered a very powerful Celtic tribe known as the Veneti, who dominated the sea coasts of Gaul and the Channel. The Veneti were expert seamen who had their tributaries among the seafaring tribes of Britain, requiring them to send auxiliaries against the Romans and to maintain their own defences against invaders. The Britons established cliff castles along the coast whose strategic importance was vital, since the Romans were thereby checked both by land and by sea. The subsequent fate of the Veneti belongs to Roman history: their great fleet was annihilated by the Romans in a terrible sea-battle fought in Morbihan Bay, thus leaving the way open for Caesar's invasion in 55 B.C.

Obviously a strong system of defence was of crucial importance to the British in their resistance to the Romans. Cliff forts would be established along the Kentish coast, and it would not be surprising to find one on the West Cliff at Folkestone. We suggest that Eadbald's castle was originally a British fort, used for defence and as a look-out post.

6 THE HISTORY OF FOLKESTONE

Caesar found the Britons ready massed on the cliffs to receive him when he arrived one morning about 9.0 a.m. off Dover. They had sighted his ships early on and gave them a rough reception, hurling javelins and rocks down from the cliffs above. So he decided to attempt a landing at an undefended place further north.

There are a few surviving traces of British hill forts and cliff forts in Kent. Caesar's Camp is the most prominent hill fort in our district, and as we suggest, the cliff fort on the Bayle was probably British. The best example is to be found on the cliff top at Dover; and if we look down from the keep of the existing Norman Castle we can easily trace the ancient ramparts from which the Britons drove off the invading Romans. In fact the present Norman Castle was established inside the ramparts of the old British fort; and since the Romans, the Saxons and the Normans used the fort in this way, it is likely that a similar plan was carried out on the West Cliff at Folkestone. But owing to the fact that the Folkestone cliff was made of greensand which was liable to slip into the sea, almost all trace of the original fort has vanished.

WATCH TOWERS

During their subsequent occupation of Britain the Romans built a watch tower or pharos inside the fort at Dover. It is still to be seen there, and they probably built another at Folkestone. In fact Gildas tells us of five watch towers in Kent, but he does not say where they were. Presumably the four Roman forts of the Saxon Shore each had one, and the fifth might easily be at Folkestone. Later historians like Harris and Hasted assumed that a watch tower had been built on Castle Hill (Caesar's Camp), but this was not a suitable place, being too far from the sea. Moreover, no evidence of such a tower has been found there.

We may get some idea of the shape and position of the original West Cliff (traditionally known as 'Bold Head'), upon which the first British fort was made, and on which the Romans may have built their tower, by studying the line of the coast as it was over two thousand years ago. The sketch in Fig. 1 which is based on a survey made in 1873 shows the submarine contours off the Folkestone coast. We know that this part of

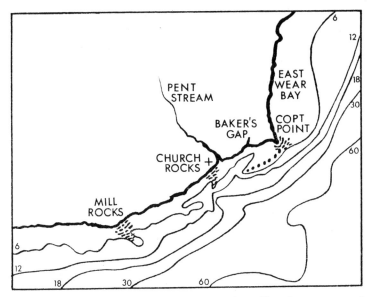

FIG. I. Contours of the sea-bed off the Folkestone shore. Note the promontory by the church rocks, and the inlet towards Baker's Gap.

Kent has been sinking into the sea at the rate of a foot a century, and so the three-fathom line would be above water level, and would in Caesar's time mark the outline of the coast. The outline is markedly different from the present one, and it shows how much of the coast has been worn away by the sea. It is clear that from the closeness of the contours at the point now known as 'Church Rocks' that here was once a steep cliff which reared its head boldly out to sea, and so provided an ideal situation for a coastal hill fort, and later, perhaps, a watch tower.

BAKER'S GAP

This cliff also protected the inlet made by the Pent stream and its little haven. The contours show also another inlet further east where another stream ran down a cleft in the cliff into the sea. We know the cleft today as 'Baker's Gap' but this is probably a popular corruption of 'Bekkr Gap'; the word 'bekkr' being an old Norse word meaning 'stream or beck' and 'gap' is Norse for 'chasm'. The stream and the cleft are still there today, but much reduced. Formerly, it was very likely

as much used as the 'sea-gate' or Pent valley, as it led to the
British settlement above. The word 'gap' like 'gate' and 'stairs'
is typical of east Kent, and they all indicate the seaways used
by the oldest inhabitants. It is no wonder they needed cliff forts
to deter pirates and invaders.

CELTIC VILLA

But to return to the early Britons. Further evidence of Celtic
habitation was revealed when the Roman villas on East Cliff
were excavated in 1924. The foundations of a Celtic villa were
found beneath the Roman villa, showing that this place was
originally a centre of Celtic life. This was a surprising discovery
since the Celts did not usually build houses of stone, but were
content to live in buildings of framed timber and wattle, roofed
with thatch. These usually leave little trace behind; but the
owner of this Celtic dwelling must have adopted the Roman
style of living in a stone house, a fact which suggests that he
was a man of wealth and influence in the district. Similar Celtic
villas have been found on the continent, and it is likely that
the family living here had some pretentions to culture and were
possibly farmers and traders.

Very few other traces of Celtic life have been found. There
have been several coins, mostly from the villa site, two swords
dredged up from the sea and a few pieces of pottery. But though
the traces of material culture are few, the Celts have left an
indelible mark on our language and on our maps. This is
evidence which has not been sufficiently investigated and
evaluated, partly because the written records do not go back
far enough to satisfy the historian. But the study of place-
names may provide valuable suggestions which should not be
ignored. Traces of the Celtic language may be found in scores
of names on the maps of Britain, for the Celtic settlers gave
names to most of the prominent features of the land and to their
early homesteads—names which have been handed down to us
through the centuries.

CELTIC PLACE NAMES

If we look at an ancient map of Kent (the older the better),
and set aside names of Saxon and later origin, we are left with
the names of the oldest settlements and of the basic features of

the county: names of rivers—Thames, Medway, Stour, Limen, Cray, Teise and Beult; names of ancient towns like Dover, Romney, Winchelsea and Chatham; features like Thanet, the Downs and the Rhee Wall; and to these we may add the names of places which the Romans latinized as Durolevum, Durobrivae, Regulbium and Rutupiae; all these have Celtic derivations; and finally, the name 'Kent' is Celtic.

If we look at our local names we shall find further signs of Celtic habitation. The words 'Pent' and 'Ford' are Celtic; 'Jacob's Mount' probably conceals a Celtic form as 'munt' is Celtic. We have already noted Bekkr Gap which probably goes further back still. In Speed's map of Kent Sugar Loaf Hill is called 'Eachborough' meaning 'horse hill'. How did it get this name? It is possibly a surviving record of the ancient cult of the White Horse. It is known that the Belgic inhabitants in south-east Britain worshipped the goddess of fertility, the 'Ga Mater' in the form of a white horse. For example, the great tribe known to the Romans as the 'Iceni' were horse worshippers, and they called themselves the 'Eachanaidh', meaning 'people of the horse'. The word 'each' (horse) appears in several local names and suggests a local cult of the horse deity. Votive models of the horse made in clay have been found in Canterbury. We recall that the white horse has long been the emblem of Kent; that Celtic chieftains issued coins stamped with the image of the horse; that horse emblems were cut in the turf of the chalk downs at Uffington and Westbury; and that the ancient ritual of the 'Hodden Horse', performed for centuries throughout Kent, is still performed in Folkestone— although nobody knows why. It is probably one of our oldest surviving rituals, and is connected with the ancient fertility cult of the Horse Goddess, Epona.

DERIVATION OF FOLKESTONE

It is pertinent to ask at this point where the name of 'Folkestone' came from. This again was probably Celtic, although it is difficult to be sure. The ancient historians of monastic times jumped to the conclusion that the name was Saxon, and meant 'the stone of the people'; and they latinized it as 'Lapis populi'. But the oldest records show the spelling as 'Folcanstan' (696), and 'Folcanstanae' (824). But 'folcan' was not the genitive form of 'folc' in Anglo-Saxon, and could not mean 'of the people'. So this derivation must be wrong. The *Oxford Dictionary of Place Names* suggests that the word means 'Folca's Stone' without explaining who Folca was. The clue to the riddle must lie in the form 'Folcan', written with an 'n'. A possible suggestion is the ancient British name 'Folgens'. There was a British prince named Folgens, and Folkestone might have been connected with him or a chieftain of the same name. If so, the early form of the word might be 'Folgensdon', the 'don' being the hill fort on the west cliff where he had a ceremonial 'stone'. After the departure of the Romans the Saxon settlers would adapt the name to 'Folcanstan', (the form recorded in 696), 'Folca' being a related Saxon name, and the word 'stan' (stone) being a reminder of the original stone. Later it was taken as the meeting place of the 'hundred'. In any case the name suggests that the place was of some political and strategic importance in Celtic times.

PILGRIM'S WAY

Furthermore, it was situated at the eastern end of the ancient pilgrim's road which connected the Channel with the ancient religious centre of Stonehenge. There was constant traffic between the continent and Kent via Folkestone on the way to Stonehenge, and had been since the Bronze Age. The road began at East Wear Bay and continued along the base of the hills; it is known as the 'terrace way' and can still be traced. It was in fact the original Pilgrim's Way which led into the heart of Wessex.

East Wear Bay was a suitable landing place for pilgrims and travellers from the continent, bound for Stonehenge. The name 'Wear' is very likely derived from the Saxon word 'weoh' meaning a 'heathen temple'. It is possible that such a temple was found in 1872 in the field close by, known as 'the Folly'. In the course of laying foundations workmen found part of a Roman hypocaust, and the remains of a Christian chapel. No one could account for this chapel unless it was the long lost chapel of St. Botolph. But close by they also found the foundations of a circular building which puzzled everybody. It might have been the 'heathen temple'—a Celtic temenos—referred to in the word 'weoh'. It was customary for the early Christians to build churches on the site of heathen temples to obliterate their memory, and this might account for the existence of St. Botolph's Chapel so far from the fishing village by the sea. It would be appropriate for the Celtic people to have a shrine close to their landing place to give thanks for a safe sea journey. Similarly we might hazard a suggestion that the site of St. Mary's Church on the West Cliff had once been the site of a Celtic temple, and so account for the building of the parish church on the heights above the town.

Behind Sugar Loaf Hill beside the ancient trackway there was a Holy Well. This was a very suitable place for a temenos, as the Celts favoured lonely places and especially springs for their shrines; and it was customary for them to throw their offerings into the waters of the well. Much of interest may still be buried in the mud below.

All that we have said of the Celtic period of occupation is largely speculation; it is bound to be so, since we have so little evidence to build on, and there has been no systematic excavation of the area. Apart from the foundations of the Celtic villa we have only a few Celtic coins—one recently discovered was stamped with the name of 'Amminus', perhaps a local 'rix'. Two Celtic swords have been dredged from East Wear Bay, and a few funerary urns and pottery shards have been found. Much has been inevitably lost in the sea . . . But if our discussion of the evidence leads to further investigation and a better understanding of an obscure period, it will have been worth while.

A piece of evidence has very recently come to light on this question. Two investigators, using special electronic devices in searching for coins and other metal objects on Castle Hill and Sugar Loaf Hill reported that they found 640 coins on the latter, one being a bronze quarter-Stater of the Celtic period, dated about 5-10 A.D., and minted in the reign of Eppillus of Kent. There were a number of Roman coins as well, chiefly of the first and second century. There were far fewer coins found on Castle Hill, and nothing older than George I.

The large quantity of coins on Sugar Loaf Hill, many of them Roman, suggests that this hill was used by the Romans as well as by the Celts. It was not a likely place to spend money, and we suggest that the coins were cast from the hill top (for luck) as an offering to Epona, the Horse Goddess; hence the ancient name of Eachborough for the hill.

The absence of Roman coins on Castle Hill seems to show conclusively that it was not used by the Romans for their watch tower, and Sugar Loaf Hill was not a likely place either. There is a need for further exploration in the near future, before the site is destroyed by future developments.

CHAPTER TWO

THE ROMANS IN FOLKESTONE

THE tradition that there had been Roman occupation in Folkestone was amply confirmed in 1924 when an important villa site was excavated in East Wear Bay just east of the Folly fields. Two years previously a slight landslip at the cliff edge had revealed a Roman drain tile projecting from the cliff and leading to a culvert which appeared to belong to a building of some size. Mr. Peden of the local museum discussed it with Mr. S. E. Winbolt, an archaeologist, who agreed to excavate the site. The Borough Council granted £150 and labour from the ranks of the unemployed for the task, and by the autumn of 1924, two large villa sites were uncovered; and after suitable arrangements were made, they were thrown open to the public, and for some years the excavations were one of the highlights of attraction for visitors to Folkestone (Plate 1).

VILLAS OF TWO PERIODS

Mr. Winbolt reported that the site contained the foundations of buildings of two different periods. The earlier villa was erected before the Roman conquest of A.D. 43, and probably belonged to a wealthy landowner of the British aristocracy. In the light of recent discoveries at Fishbourne, near Chichester, where the place of a British 'rix' named Cogidumnus was unearthed, we wonder whether our villa was the home of Folkestone's 'rix'. It was built on a Romano-Celtic model, examples of which have been found on the continent, and it seems to suggest that the owner had already adopted the Roman style of living. The villa walls had been constructed of local ragstone and it had several rooms. It had evidently been commandeered for military use by the Romans on account of its strategic position; after a few years it was demolished and replaced by a much larger building, some time before A.D. 100. Furthermore, another separate villa had been built at right angles to the first.

The main Roman villa, facing south-east, was constructed on a symmetrical plan, roughly E-shaped, with two equal wings projecting at either end, and with a small flight of steps in the centre, leading to the centre of a corridor and to the chief sitting room with its tesselated floor. Two corridors, each nine feet wide, ran on either side of the suite of rooms forming the main block of the building, one end of which had been rebuilt to provide a hypocaust and a cold plunge bath. At the end of either wing was a stair-case chamber, so the two wings probably had an upper storey, while the centre block was of the bungalow type with lofty rooms. Both wings ended in rooms with bow-fronted projections. This building was the larger and more elaborate of the two and was probably designed as the residence of an important official.

The second villa, separated from the other by a garden or courtyard, was probably used by the subordinate officers and their families. It consisted of one long block of rooms, flanked by corridors seven feet wide on either side, and serving as a means of communication between the living rooms. At the eastern end was a hypocaust, bath and furnace. Both villas were strongly built on footings of sea stones resting on the gault, with a filling of Roman rubble of mortar, tiles and stones. They were faced with dressed stones from the local quarries. In all there were fifty-six rooms in the two villas, counting all the corridors, bathrooms and offices, so providing accommodation for a considerable number of people. There may be other Roman buildings nearby, still undiscovered, and stretching as far back as the Folly, where another Roman building was found in 1872, as we saw before.

The evidence provided by pottery and coins found on the site showed that the two villas were inhabited from about A.D. 100 until after A.D. 350. They were not damaged by fire or otherwise destroyed, but simply evacuated by the inhabitants, probably owing to the growing threat of Saxon inroads from the sea.

THE FINDS

Mr. Winbolt reported that most of the objects usually found on Romano-British sites were discovered. There was Samian ware dating from A.D. 100 to 350, but most plentifully of the second century. Coins ranged from Augustus to Maxentius, but the largest number were of the Constantine period. There were many stone querns for grinding corn by hand, window glass, iron nails and tools, some bronze objects and silver ornaments. Also, British coins, British burial urns, and British ornaments of bronze and silver, obviously relics of the British inhabitants of the pre-Roman days, were discovered. Altogether this was a rich and important site.

THEIR PURPOSE

The first question which arises is why the Roman villas were built here and what purpose they served. Fortunately, some unequivocal evidence was provided by the discovery of several large tiles stamped with the initials CL:BR, which were the sign of the marines serving with the Roman fleet. The Romans had to maintain a permanent navy in the channel, based on Boulogne (Gessoriacum), for the protection of their troopships, transports and cornships. Wherever the Roman marines were quartered, they constructed barracks and forts, as required, and they stamped the large heavy tiles used for supporting the floors of hypocausts, with these initials. They were short for 'Classis Britannica' meaning 'British Fleet'. They have been found at Dover and Richborough, two other naval bases as well as at Boulogne. In the later period of the occupation when the threat of attack from Saxon invaders grew, the defences on the British coast were increased. In the third century a range of nine forts was built along the coast from Hunstanton to Porchester, and put under the command of an official known as 'The Count of the Saxon Shore'. The forts in Kent were Lympne, Dover, Richborough, and Reculver. Folkestone was not one of them as we know from the fact that it was not named in the official Roman list. But the presence of the tell-tale tiles indicates that these buildings at Folkestone were part of the defence system. We do not know what part they played, but we may hazard a suggestion.

A SIGNALLING BASE

They were not villas in the ordinary sense of domestic dwellings occupied by a wealthy farmer, as were Bignor or Lullingstone. In fact the Romans discouraged the settlement of villas too near the coast. They were more probably buildings used by a small military or naval detachment, connected with coastal defence. Mr. Winbolt went so far as to suggest that they were the headquarters of the Count of the Saxon Shore himself; but it would be unlikely for a high-ranking officer to reside at a minor establishment. His place would be at Dover or Richborough where his main forces were, and some inferior officer would occupy our building. We suggest that the settlement was really a signalling base, to send messages of possible attack to the military centres on either hand. Copt point would be an ideal spot for a look-out base (as it still is today); and the British fort on the West Cliff, which protruded further out to sea in those times, would be a good site for a beacon tower to send warning to Dover and Lympne. And so the age-old tradition of the Roman beacon tower would be verified. It is to be noted that there appears to have been a denser habitation on the east than on the west of Folkestone. This may be explained by the fact that the Warren with its shallower shore protected by the Copt Point provided better landing conditions than the Stade, which has always been more exposed to the south-west winds.

ROMANS AND BRITONS

What effect would Roman occupation have on the native population? It seems that in most areas, after the initial conflict, Roman mercenaries fraternized easily with them. The Romans might bring a few luxuries—wine, pottery, glass, jewellery and metalware—and introduce new ideas to the people. The latter would continue in their farming and fishing occupations and barter their produce for the coveted luxuries. In the later period a few Britons might venture to pay a visit to Durovern (Canterbury) to see the forum and the amphitheatre; but for the most part Britons and Romans lived side by side, enjoying a slightly more sophisticated way of life in return for Roman taxes and protection. Romans and Britons worshipped similar gods and tolerated one another's religious cults. They intermarried and they were even buried side by side, as evidence showed from a cemetery excavated at Cheriton in 1948. There British and Roman burial urns were found together beside the old Roman road at Cheriton Street where there must have been a small settlement at a road junction.

The Roman period ended for Folkestone's inhabitants some

time shortly before A.D. 368 when the great incursion of Picts, Scots and Saxons began. The Roman forces were simply withdrawn from the station. Certainly the Roman buildings were evacuated peacefully, and the natives sought safety inland, leaving the area relatively uninhabited for many years.

One question remains to be answered: why is Folkestone never mentioned in the official documents of the period which have come down to us? The place is entirely omitted from the Antonine Itineraries, the Notitia Dignitatum and the Peuteringer Tables. The answer is probably a very simple one. Other towns in Kent are mentioned, such as Richborough (Rutupiae), Dubris (Dover) and Portus Lemanis (Lympne). But these were all ports situated at the seaward end of Roman roads, and they all provided a harbourage for the Roman ships. The Roman transports and cornships could be moored under the very walls of these towns because there was deep water provided by the various rivers flowing out to sea. Folkestone had no such river and could not offer a deep enough anchorage for large ships, and therefore played a minor role in Roman history. But raiders and pirates could effect a landing in their light boats, and so constituted a grave danger. A small contingent of marines was therefore established here and a signalling post maintained to watch the coast and to send messages to Dover and Lympne.

CHAPTER THREE

THE SAXON PERIOD

THE history of Britain in the next 300 years is confused, what with inroads from Saxon pirates, attempts at restoration of control by the Romans, and their final withdrawal in A.D. 410. The history of Folkestone in these years is virtually a blank, and one can see why when one considers the terrible reputation which the Saxon marauders had. Even the Romans had a fearful respect for the attackers as we learn from a letter written by Sidonius Apollinaris, a Gaul, to a Roman naval commander on patrol duty in the channel. He writes:

> 'A messenger arrived when I was on the point of ending my letter . . . He tells me you had just given the signal to sail to your fleet, and that you were patrolling the Channel against the light curved Saxon raiding ships. They are all brigands and they teach and learn piracy. So you must always be on the alert. This enemy is more ferocious than any other; he comes unexpectedly and if you are prepared he slips away. Shipwrecks do not terrify them and they are used to the perils of the sea. For whereas a storm prevents observation and puts us off our guard, the hope of a surprise attack leads them to risk their lives among the waves and the rocks. Moreover, before they return home, it is their barbarous custom to drown every tenth captive (such is their deplorable religion) by casting lots over the doomed victims. With such vows they bind themselves and placate their gods with victims.'

The Britons appealed again and again for help against the raiders, but the Romans were themselves sorely pressed and the Emperor Honorius told them they must look to their own defence. The raids went on; Picts and Scots and Saxons combined to make devastating inroads.

BRITISH POLITICS

It was at this time that two parties emerged in the former Roman province. There were the Romano-Britons who had enjoyed prosperity under Roman rule, and had adopted the Roman style of living, and, for the most part, were responsible for the government and administration of the country. The other party consisted of the original Celtic stock dwelling mostly in the west, cherishing their ancient ways, and wishing to regain control of the province. A leader emerged from this party named Vortigern, whose influence was to dominate the scene for the next thirty years. Under his leadership the British party defeated the Picts and Scots who were harrying the north and east coasts; but by 440 new inroads by the Saxons caused the Romano-British party to appeal to the Roman general in Gaul, Aëtius, for assistance. But the Romans were too busy defending themselves to give help. Vortigern stepped in once more and made a treaty with certain Saxon warrior bands to defend the coasts of Britain against the Picts and Scots. These warriors were known as 'feudatories', that is, mercenary troops who were engaged at a price to fight for any leader willing to employ them; and the feudatories chosen by Vortigern, had previously seen service with the Romans and were familiar with Roman military tactics. They were led by two chieftains, Hengist and Horsa, who had left their native territory, traditionally from Jutland on the continent and gone into exile.

So according to Bede, in 449 Hengist and his brother Horsa came to protect the British coasts under an arrangement with Vortigern, by which they were granted the island of Thanet as a base and a home for their families. Archaeological records show that the Saxons settled even further inland on the banks of the Stour below Canterbury. It was a fatal step for the Britons as the feudatories had a bridgehead in the country. For a few years the arrangement was satisfactory, Hengist's mercenaries and their families receiving payment in kind for their services in repulsing invaders; but after a time their demands became excessive, and a quarrel was forced on the Britons. A number of battles were fought in the years 455 and 456, at Crayford, Aylesford, and finally on the sea-shore in south-east Kent. In the battle of Aylesford Horsa was killed, and, according to Bede, 'Horsa . . . was buried in the eastern parts of Kent, where a monument, bearing his name, is still in existence.' After this the Saxons withdrew for some years until they could return with reinforcements.

A SAXON CEMETERY

We have recounted some of this early history to see whether
there is any evidence of these struggles near Folkestone. One
might expect that there were skirmishes on the plateau behind
the village, between the North Downs and the sea. One piece of
evidence was accidentally discovered in 1907 at Killick's
Corner. To quote the Official Guide to Folkestone Museum
and Art Gallery (1927):

> 'In 1907 while the road at Dover Hill was being widened the
> workmen came upon an ancient burial ground. Many skeletons
> were found, and the interment would appear in nearly all cases
> to have been made in such a manner that the faces were turned
> towards the rising sun. It is believed this burial ground which
> is on a southern slope was Jutish and dated about 600 A.D. The
> practice of these people would appear to have been to dig down
> to the chalk and then merely cut a bed for the deceased, and it
> is probable that to this fact is due the good preservation of these
> bones after thirteen hundred years of interment.
>
> 'There were many interesting relics including:— A large
> sword; many smaller swords or daggers; spear heads; metal
> bosses to shields; a bit which had been part of the harness of a
> favourite horse; strings of amber beads; bracelets, bone hair-
> pins, metal tweezers; a brooch inlaid and faced with gold, and
> inset with white shell and garnets. A complete female skeleton;
> an earthen flask.'

Apart from the female skeleton, this looks like a company
of warriors who had fallen in battle; and in any case the
situation of the site on the steep slope of a hill suggests an
emergency burial ground. It is probable that we have evidence
here of one of the minor battles fought in the early Saxon period
at a date nearer A.D. 500.

And what about Horsa's grave and monument? No such
monument now exists in east Kent, but there may be a pointer
to its former situation in some of the ancient maps of Kent.
Symondson's map (1596) notes a place called 'Hawsborow'
close to East Wear Bay; and the name 'Hawborow' in Speed's
map apparently relates to a site on Copt Point. In the town
records there is a deed of gift dated 1573, of a piece of land at
'Horseborough', which is located near the Folly on East Cliff.
The estate map made in 1697 for Jacob des Bouverie shows a
field called 'Hasborough Field' and another called 'Hasborough
Hill and bushes' which is the hillock on Copt Point. We still

have a modern row of houses called 'Hasborough Road' on East Cliff. It seems likely that Hawsborow was the little mount on which Martello Tower No. 3 still stands. It is here that we might have a sporting chance of finding evidence of Horsa's grave—that is if the builders of the Tower did not destroy it.

A SHIP BURIAL

And while we are considering early burials it is worth recalling the mysterious entry in Leland: 'and this Lord Clynton's grand father had there of a poor man a boote almost ful of antiquities of pure gold and sylver.' Allowing for differences of spelling we might conclude that the 'boote' was a 'boat', and very likely the 'poore man' had stumbled on the relics of a Saxon Ship burial like the famous Sutton Hoo ship burial. Whose was it? Was it Horsa's? What happened to all those gold and silver antiquities? If they had been preserved they would tell us much about the Saxons in Folkestone. The discovery must have been made about 1500, and the jewels claimed as treasure trove by the Lord Clinton of the day. It is just possible that they may still be in existence. But here again we have no certain knowledge of the events and we are thrown back upon surmise.

We know nothing about what happened in our district during the next two centuries. There were constant battles between the British and the encroaching Saxons, but by 500 Kent was an established Saxon kingdom. In 597 King Ethelbert was converted to Christianity by Augustine, and the work of the Church began in bringing letters, learning and a more civilized way of life.

ST. EANSWYTHE

King Ethelbert was succeeded by his son, Eadbald, who, after his conversion to Christianity, founded a nunnery for his daughter, Eanswythe, in A.D. 630 at Folkestone. This is the first time that Folkestone is mentioned in recorded history. Eanswythe had been educated in a convent on the continent and at Canterbury and was a devout Christian. She must have been a remarkable young woman with a strong will of her own, as her father soon discovered. When she became of marriageable age and returned to her father's court, she steadfastly refused to take a husband, in defiance of her father's wishes. He wanted her to marry a Northumbrian King, so forming a dynastic alliance: but she had a poor idea of marriage to the Saxon males of her day—and who can blame her when we consider her delicate religious upbringing and the crudeness of Saxon life. She rejected a political marriage to a mortal husband and longed for 'the embraces of a heavenly and immortal spouse'; and in order to worship him, she begged her father to be allowed to build an oratory for herself. She had her way, and took to the religious life.

THE NUNNERY

In building her nunnery, the first in England, she deliberately sought a place remote from habitation, and finally chose a spot close to the edge of the West Cliff at Folkestone. We can imagine her little church and its domestic buildings standing on the cliff which projected out to sea. Eanswythe thought that her nunnery was safe enough; and so it was in her time. But in succeeding centuries the sea undermined the cliff and so destroyed it. We can still see today how far out the land went if we stand on the Leas on a sunny day at low water with a fresh breeze to ruffle the sea. Where the deep water begins the sea looks blue; but where the waves have ruffled the sandy shallows the water looks a sandy green colour. The shallows mark the contours of the seashore as it was some fifteen hundred years ago (see sketch p.7).

Eadbald's castle or fort, which was probably the old British fort renewed and strengthened, lay a little to the west of the nunnery. It consisted of earthen ramparts with wooden palisades. Eanswythe's nunnery, too, would be built of wood, and was perhaps rebuilt later in stone. None of these exist now, but we may trace the landward side of the castle ramparts by walking along the Parade, down Bail Street and up George Lane, where the land rises quite steeply. This is the northern end of the rampart, or the Bayle, as the Normans later called the outer works of the fort.

THE TOWN DYKE

To return to Eanswythe. She appears to have been a woman of resource, as she supervised the building of her church and the nunnery. She probably directed the labours of her servants who were British serfs. The nunnery lacked a water supply, so according to the legend in Capgrave's *Nova Legenda*, she conveyed the water of a spring at Sweeton in the neighbourhood of Castle Hill, to her nunnery. At that time the country at the base of the hills was marshland, but she had a dyke made to carry the spring water all the way to her nunnery on the cliff. The dyke had to cross the Pent stream and the adjacent marshes, so a small aqueduct was built to bring the water to the higher ground behind the present Guildhall Street to the Bayle. For centuries it was the town water supply and was known as the 'Town Dyke', and fed the Bayle pond. Eanswythe devoted herself to helping the poor and training her novitiates, and her nunnery became well known as a centre of Christian learning. She died in 640 and was later canonized for her charitable works and saintly life. She was buried in her chapel.

After her death her nuns carried on her work until the nunnery was in danger of falling into the sea; there is also a suggestion that the nunnery had been attacked by the Danes. However, the nuns transferred themselves and St. Eanswythe's relics to St. Peter's church nearby, which had been built by Eadbald. There they established a new nunnery and carried on her work. The Saxon Kings were very generous in their bequests to the religious foundations in Kent. In 70 years no fewer than eight houses were founded in east Kent. The nobles followed the royal pattern and we have evidence of bequests to Folkestone made by King Wihtred in 649; by the Saxon Thane Abba in 835; and by Duke Oswulf in 844. This wealth was probably expended in building a stone chapel for the nunnery, a dormitory and other offices, and in enriching the buildings with gold and silver vessels. The richer the place became the more tempting it was to raiders, and it was ultimately attacked and reduced to ruins by the Danes.

In 927 King Athelstan restored the church and nunnery once more, and his Charter reads as follows:

'For the reverence and honour of the archpriest Wulfhelm, I grant to the Church of Christ at Canterbury, the land belonging to me in Kent, situated on the sea, called Folcestan, where formerly there was a monastery and convent of holy virgins, where also St. Eanswida was buried. Wherefore I, Aethelstane, monarch of all Britain, thought upon that place and on the service of Christ and of St. Mary His Mother which of old was carried on in the same place before it was destroyed by the Pagans, and have given it to the Church of Christ in order that the service which used to be performed there may be restored.'

The relics of St. Eanswythe were transferred to the new church, as Goscelinus tells us, and the work of the nunnery continued for a further 150 years. But in 1052 it was again reduced to ruins by Earl Godwin who ravaged the coast of Kent out of spite as a result of a quarrel with the King. For years the ruins were left desolate until in 1095 another completely new church was founded by the new Norman Lord of the Manor, Nigel de Muneville. With it he built, not a nunnery, but a Priory for Benedictine monks. But before we consider the subsequent developments in the Norman period, we must return to Saxon Folkestone.

SAXON FOLKESTONE

The presence of the nunnery and the castle encouraged fishermen and farmers to settle in the valley below. So a new Folkestone began soon after A.D. 630 under the protection of St. Eanswythe. We are reminded of this by looking at the seal of the Mayor of Folkestone, which shows a standing image of the Saint dressed as an Abbess and crowned, with two fishes sporting alongside. Thus the seal records the origin of the Saxon town.

This was still no more than a small hamlet, consisting of a collection of huts on the banks of the Pent stream and the foreshore. A track led up to the Bayle on the line of the present High Street and turned south towards the church and castle. We must remember that the original settlement was situated further out to sea than the present fishmarket, and the Stade extended between the headlands of the West Cliff and East Cliff. Inland the Pent valley was filled with trees and bushes, and most of the countryside was well wooded except where a few farms had been cut out of the wild. Nowadays the whole area is covered with houses: but if we imagine all the buildings to be trees, we shall get some idea of the appearance of the district.

Farms usually have a very long history as they are sited

where the land is arable. Successive invaders tend to occupy the old sites which may go back even to the Bronze Age. We have no knowledge at present of the early history of our farms, but maybe Walton Farm was run by a British family, known to the Saxons as 'weallas' ('Welshmen'); hence Weal-tun. Park Farm was protected by a moat, and was one of the largest and oldest in the district. It was hewn out of the forest or 'park' which covered the Folkestone Plain. Ingles Farm, Plain Farm and Oaks Farm are probably very old too, but it is not until the Domesday Survey that we get a glimpse of the social background of the district.

Fishing and farming were the main occupations of the ordinary folk of Folkestone, no matter who owned the land. We get a vivid picture of conditions for the ordinary man of the day from Aelfric's *Colloquies*:

> *Ploughman:* Oh, my lord, hard do I work. I go out at daybreak driving the oxen to the field, and I yoke them to the plough. Nor is the winter ever so hard that I dare loiter at home, for fear of my lord; but, the oxen yoked and the ploughshare and coulter fastened to the plough, every day I must plough a full acre or more.
>
> Hast thou any comrade?
>
> *Ploughman:* I have a boy driving the oxen with an iron goad, and he also is hoarse with cold and shouting.
>
> What more dost thou do in the day?
>
> *Ploughman:* Verily then I do more. I must fill the bin of the oxen with hay, and water them, and carry out the dung. Hard work it is, hard work it is . . .

We are apt to forget the labours of the humble poor so eloquently expressed here. The records deal mostly with the owners of the manor; and so we learn that the manors of Folkestone and Walton were originally given by Eadbald to the Nunnery, but in 927 they belonged to Christ's Church at Canterbury. For a time Earl Godwin possessed them.

At the Conquest they were given to Bishop Odo, half-brother of William the Conqueror. This suggests that William attached considerable importance to the barony for its value and its strategic position; he therefore took it from the Church and put it under his brother's protection. Some years later when Odo fell into disgrace, he was deprived of his lands which were given to another of the King's supporters.

PART II

THE MIDDLE PERIOD

CHAPTER FOUR

FROM THE NORMANS TO THE TUDORS

THE Doomsday entry tells us that William D'Arcy held the Barony of Folkestone in 1086, and he was a Norman. It was William the Conqueror's policy in the early years to confirm the English landowners in their possessions and to govern through them; but the importance of the barony was such that he probably thought it desirable to have it in Norman hands. We get a glimpse of the barony from the record in Doomsday Book:

> 'William D'Arcy holds Fulchestan. In the reign of Edward (the Confessor) it was rated at 40 sowlings: it is now rated at 39 (A sowling is about 160 acres). The arable land is one hundred and twenty carucates (ploughlands). In the demesne there are two hundred and nine villeins, and 83 borderers (bondsmen). Among all they have forty-five carucates. There are five churches, from which the archbishop has fifty-five shillings. There are three servants, and seven mills of nine pounds twelve shillings. There are one hundred acres of meadow. Wood for the pannage of forty hogs. Earl Godwin held this manor.'

Here follows a list of subtenants with their holdings: seven Normans—Hugh FitzWilliam, Walter de Appeville, Bernard de St. Owen, Walter FitzEngelbert, Eudo, Baldric and Richard; and three who were probably Saxons—Alured, Wesman, and Alured Dapifer (Purveyor). Some Saxons were evidently allowed to keep their holdings. The Doomsday record continues:

> 'All Fulchestan, in the time of King Edward the Confessor, was worth one hundred and ten pounds; when he (William D'Arcy) received it forty pounds, now what he has in demesne is worth one hundred pounds; what the knights hold above-mentioned together, is worth forty-five pounds and ten shillings.'

The change in value of the barony was probably due partly to the depredations of Earl Godwin who attacked the coastal towns in 1052, and partly to the unsettled conditions in the years following the Conquest. But by 1086 the farms had recovered and the district seems to have been fairly prosperous. There were about 300 men living on the demesne, and with a similar number of women there were about 600 adults.

BARONIAL DUTIES

William D'Arcy and his successors in the barony held their lands from the king by knight's service. That is, they were required to equip and supply a certain number of men at arms for the defence of the country; in their case, they had to send their men to stand on guard for a stated period at Dover Castle. Their sub-tenants had to provide their quota according to the size of their tenures. The men were allocated to a tower in the castle which was named after the Baron, and the Averanches Tower still commemorates this fact. As the Baron had his chief residence on the Bayle at Folkestone it was called 'caput baroniae'; and, as the headquarters of the barony, it was thus singled out as a place of importance. Moreover, the Baron held jurisdiction in three courts at which his tenants were compelled to appear, and he collected fees and fines which he kept for himself. In studying these records we should remember that they are concerned with the farmlands and woods behind Folkestone, as well as the fishing community by the sea.

THIRTEENTH CENTURY

We are given another glimpse of the Folkestone district from a document dated 1263 in the reign of Henry III. The document is a record of an enquiry ordered by the King into the lands and tenements of Matilda Averanche, formerly wife of Hamo de Crevecoeur. As no maps, plans or surveys existed in those times, it was necessary to ask several important officials of the district to testify under oath to the ownership and value of the lands. The list of officials included Sir Henry Hauerenq, Kt., Richard Doning, William the Reeve, Ralph the Reeve, Richard Herbert, William Robert, William Cuniculus, Richard de Wingate, John de Cudham, Simon Clerk, Richard Waroman, Peter de Ecclesia and Humphrey de Embroc. These names recall a time when a man was known chiefly by his work or his local district. They testified that:

'Hamo de Creveqer held in this demesne pertaining to the manor of Folcestane, 825 acres of arable land, pasture and meadow, of the inheritance of the said Matilda, and they set each acre upon the whole at 4d. per annum, the sum whereof in money is £13 15s., of which 710 acres are in Folcstane, and 115 in Nouhinton. They say also, that there are £32 2s. 9d. of rent of assizes in Folcestane.'

Another statement made before 'Robert de Ludeham, clerk of our Lord the King, sent for this purpose by precept of our said Lord, the King' gave fuller details of the extent of the manor, as follows:

'There is a capital messuage there, sufficiently well built, enclosed with a stone wall, of which no extent can be made, because it can scarcely be sustained for 40s. per annum. There is a dovecot within the said enclosure, with the herbage of the court, and worth by the year, 18d. There is a small garden, worth, with the herbage, per annum, 3s. And there are three very poor watermills, worth, per annum, over and above their maintenance, 30s. And there are certain quarries, worth per annum, 20s. And there is a certain custom of those passing the sea, and it is worth 6s. 8d. And there is liberty of wreck, and no extent can be made of it, because it happens casually.'

The document then goes into exact details of all the various farms in the barony, and is very long. We give the substance of the account in brief:

'At Valetune (Walton) there was a barton, a garden with apples and herbage, and certain fields attached to the farm: at Bartonsgate 42 acres, at Polecherche, la Redelond, Quedwele and Peneforlang 163 acres; at Chalencroft 100 acres, at Stodwey-Super-Le-Dune 32 acres, and pasture for bullocks under Falese.

'There was a Park, enclosed by a hedge, containing in circuit about a league and a half, a mowing meadow of 22 acres, ten acres of underwood, pasture for 100 animals (if the deer be removed), three fishponds, and 50 acres covered with oaks and large white thorns, which, if they should be felled and sold, each acre would be worth six marks.

'Herstling wood contained 40 acres, Reindene wood 150 acres; at Terlingham farm including Bertongate, Rumfeld, La Merlinge and Bartonsdane there was a total of 127 acres. In addition, the farm held 90 acres at Kingsdane, Ruchnolle, Bernesdane, North Knole and Kellingsdane; there were a further 80 acres of arable land at Chalkedfeld and Golthorne, Newelond, Holmed, and under Oxegrove. In the fields of Bromefeld and Gorst there were a further 41 acres, and the broom and furze might be cut every seven years. On La Dune, six acres in one place, and in another place a pasture for 200

sheep called 'Mirabel'; and there was a windmill there, worth
with its suit, 40 shillings.

'At Newetun there was a messuage, weakly built, in a small
court and small garden; it had 60 acres of arable land in
Furland, under La Dune, in Belcheberche and La Ponde. It
also had 6 acres of meadow, 42 acres of pasture, a wood of 30
acres and one other wood.'

The document ends here and gives no further details of the
district, and, disappointingly, says nothing about the fishing
community: but it does tell us the names of some of the sub-
tenants: Sir Nicholas de Crioll, Sir William de Wiltune,
Henry de Evering, John de Eversley, John de Boyntune,
William de la Sale, Humphrey de Enbroc, Abbot of St.
Radegund's, Walter de Detlinge, Ambros de Laverham, the
Master of Domus Dei of Ospringe, and Master of the Hospital
at Swynefeld. These were the aristocracy of the time and all
were, presumably, Normans. It is interesting to see how many
of the ancient names still survive today. The emphasis in the
document is on farming and it shows how a landowner derived
his income from the land. By the end of the thirteenth century
the balance will have changed somewhat, and the fishing
community will have grown in importance.

FEUDAL SYSTEM

But first we should take a closer look at the structure of
society at this period, so as to compare the state of affairs
generally in Kent with that in Folkestone. Apart from the
King who owned all the land, there were two great powers
who 'held' their land from the king in return for services
rendered. The knights and barons held their estates in return
for military service and for their responsibility for organizing
the 'fyrd' or 'home guard' when required by the king. The
Church, which owned over half the land in Kent, was another
powerful body whose influence touched every member of the
community. The common people were attached to the manors
from which the lords and the Church derived their income,
and were required to give manual labour to the former and to
pay tithes to the latter. The labourers, called villeins, borders,
or cotters, supported themselves by the produce of the common
lands which they worked on the open field system; but they
were bound to give so many days' labour to the manor farms in

return for a cottage and a share of the common lands. There were also freemen (or burgesses) who were exempt from these labours, and serfs who were at the bottom of the social scale. The villeins were not allowed to buy or sell or to give their children in marriage without the lord's consent and paying a fee. No man could leave the manor or sell his labour elsewhere. This was the feudal system as it operated at the beginning of the Norman period, but by the beginning of the thirteenth century a loosening of the regulations took place. The king found it more convenient to hire mercenaries instead of exacting knight's service, and accepted money payment instead. Similarly, the lords of the manors preferred to pay labourers instead of relying on personal service on the land, although it might still be exacted. Money was the solvent which began to change the social picture; it is known as 'commutation' of service and it paved the way towards a freer and more enterprising form of society. Eventually villeins could become freemen by a further payment of money to the lord of the manor, known as 'manumission', which abolished all remaining feudal dues and obligations.

We know that the manor of Folkestone was one of the largest and most prosperous in Kent. As a fishing village Folkestone was supplying a valuable food product in great demand by the Church and by the population generally. It is very likely that the natives obtained their freedom quite early, but there are no records to tell us the social structure of the village, or how many freemen there were. By 1300 the neighbouring towns of Hythe and Dover were boroughs governed by their burgesses or freemen. Hythe had a population of at least 1,000; Sandwich had 2,000; Canterbury had 2,500, and Dover about 1,200. It is reasonable to suppose that Folkestone also had its burgesses carrying on a useful trade in fish and having trading contacts with ports on both sides of the Channel. They would press for privileges similar to those enjoyed by the neighbouring towns, and there is a record that King Stephen (1135–1154), exempted them from customs and other dues. The Charter, translated from the Latin, reads:

'Stephen, King of England, to all his officers throughout England, Normandy, Bulloyon, and the parts of the sea, greeting:— I command that my men of Folkestone be as fully

quit of Tol and Passage, and all custom throughout the land
as my men of Dover have been so that no outrage or injury
be done to them. And therefore let no one henceforth unjustly
disquiet them under forfeiture of ten pounds. Witnesses Robt.de
Vere. Hugh Bigod. Turgis de Abrinces.'

Unfortunately this document is now lost, but it is evidence
of the growing importance of trade in the community. Their
position was not such as to secure them a place among the
Cinque Ports at an early date, probably because they did not
possess a safe harbour and did not rank as a port like Dover.
But by the end of the thirteenth century they were enlisted as
a limb of Dover, and were required to supply their quota to
the King's fleet for travel, transport or military expeditions.

FOLKESTONE BECOMES A MARKET TOWN

Further evidence of their growing prosperity may be seen in
the grant of a market every Thursday, through the offices of
the Lord Justiciar, Jeffrey Fitz-Peter in 1205, and this was confirmed by charter in 1215. In 1349 Sir John de Segrave
obtained another weekly market on Tuesdays; and in 1390
Sir John de Clinton obtained the grant of a Wednesday market
and a yearly fair on St. Giles's day. These markets reveal the
growing importance of the place and its status as a market
town. The Lords of the Manor who obtained them were not
entirely altruistic, since they derived an income from them.
Apart from fishing one of the staple industries was the quarry-
ing of ragstone for the building of churches, harbours, castles
and walls. Many of the churches of east Kent were built of
Folkestone stone. The quarries belonged to the Lord of the
Manor.

KING JOHN

In passing we might note that in 1213 Folkestone became the
scene of King John's resistance to the Pope. John had refused
to accept the Pope's nominee for the Archbishopric of Canterbury, and at the Pope's command, Philip Augustus, King
of France, was preparing to invade England. John made
Folkestone his headquarters and presumably resided on the
Bayle; but after further negotiations he submitted to the
Pope's will, and even voluntarily surrendered his kingdom to
Pandulph, the Papal Legate, receiving it back as a fief of the

Papacy. Nevertheless, in 1216, Philip made a disastrous attack on the Cinque Ports and burned the town and church at Folkestone.

THE CHARTER

Folkestone's growing importance may be seen in the part assigned to it by Sir Stephen de Pencester, Lord Warden of the Cinque Ports. In 1299 he recorded the obligations of each of the ports in providing ships for the King's navy, and he stipulated that Folkestone should supply seven boats, each manned by twenty men and a boy. He seems to have overestimated the town's capacity since it seems that it never supplied more than one boat at a time. Eventually Folkestone was designated a 'limb' of Dover and given its Charter of Incorporation in 1313. By this charter it gained a considerable measure of self-government. The burgesses were required to elect a Mayor, a Bailiff, and twelve Jurats from the freemen of the town. The Corporation held its own courts, and townsmen were exempt from attendance at the hundred and shire courts. There was a Court of Record held every fifteen days, and a Court of Requests for the recovery of small debts. The Mayor and Jurats even had power over life and death, and were required to execute their own criminals.

But in the early days the Corporation fell under the despotic influence of the Lords of the Manor, and at first it was little more than a local body required to enforce their edicts and carry out their behests without restraint or even without protest. With the decline of feudal power, the independence of the Corporation increased, and they were able to exploit more fully their peculiar privileges.

One was that the seamen of the Cinque Ports were declared to be 'free of lastage, tallage, passage, kaysage, rivage, ponsage and wreck'. These were important matters to sailors and traders, exempting them from all sorts of dues and restrictions. They were also 'lovecope-free', that is, able to trade unhindered by any monopoly or merchant guild. The portsmen sometimes took an unfair advantage over other seamen, and from this disputes arose.

One of the causes of contention was the right of 'den and strond' by which the Cinque-portsmen were permitted to dry their nets and to sell their catches of fish at Yarmouth and other nearby ports. The local fishermen not surprisingly objected and although measures were taken to avoid conflict, troubles often broke out leading to bloodshed. Folkestone men were sometimes involved.

TRADE

The privilege of trading unhindered with the continent was a profitable source of wealth, especially the export of wool, and the importing of wines, cloth and luxury goods. When opportunity occurred Folkestone seamen frequently attacked foreign merchant ships and confiscated their cargoes. This was piracy, and when foreign governments protested, the king sometimes had to pay damages. These piratical ventures invited reprisals from the French, and in 1378 the town was pillaged and burnt. Towards the end of the fourteenth century the portsmen lost control of the Channel, and Rye, Winchelsea, Hythe and Folkestone were attacked in turn. During the next century the English gained control once more, and in 1467 a Folkestone boat seized a Spanish vessel with a cargo of wine and other goods valued at £533 of contemporary money—about £10,000 of modern money. In various sea encounters Folkestone sailors came to be noted for their courage, skill and ruthlessness. We are reminded of Chaucer's Shipman, who 'If that he faught, and hadde the hyer hond, By water he sente hem hoom to every lond.' On the whole Folkestone's fortunes improved during this period and continued into the sixteenth century.

EVIDENCE OF GROWING WEALTH

Surviving wills and inventories show that there was a considerable number of fairly wealthy townsmen enjoying property and the comforts of the times. The fishing families usually held part shares in several boats, thereby reducing the impact of loss at sea. They also owned plots of land and small farms in which they invested their money, there being no banks for safe keeping. And we should remember that the fishermen were always ready to turn to farming at certain seasons of the year. Some of them could afford luxuries such as silver spoons, silver buckles, pewter table ware and handsome gowns. They

were very generous to their parish church and reveal a piety
in keeping with the religious feeling of the times.

WILLS

To illustrate this we will quote details from a few wills from
the latter end of this period. In 1465 Thomas Newsole left 6/8d
to the High Altar for tithes, 6/8d to the Vicar and 4d to each
of the three clerks at the Parish Church. He gave 4d to each of
the Lights of St. James, St. George, St. Christopher and St.
Stephen, and to the Holy Cross in the Chancel of the Blessed
Mary. To John Noold he gave a flew net and a shot net; and
he ordered all his tenements, barns, lodges and lands, together
with the fourth part of a batelle (small boat) called the John,
the fourth of half of another batelle called the Eanswythe, the
fourth of a batelle called the 'Little Sprotter' to be sold, and
the money dispensed for engaging a priest to celebrate in the
church for his soul, his parents and all faithful departed, to the
amount of 10 marks; and another 10 marks to be devoted 'to a
certain window (to be new made) on the south side of the
church, opposite the altar of St. George'.

Women also left considerable property in their wills and
gave instructions for their burial. Thus Joan Cheveler, in 1465,
ordered her body to be buried before the image of St. Christopher in the Parish Church. She left 12d for the High Altar and
20/- for the repair of the church, 4d for the Light of St.
Christopher, 12d to the Light of Corpus Christi and 4d for
the Holy Cross in the chancel of St. Nicholas. She ordered
4 torches to burn about her body on the day of her burial, and
left money for the repair of Newyngton Church, and 'to the
Honour of God and the maintanance of divine service in
Padelysworth Church'. Thomas Chapman (1490) left his
daughter Joan two silver spoons and a red girdle harnessed
with silver which was her mother's; and to Alice, his other
daughter, two silver spoons and a feather bed which was her
mother's. He ordered his horses, cows and six sheep to be sold
and 20/- in his purse used to pay his debts.

In the next century we find still more evidence of property
and growing wealth. John Ingram in 1544 left to his wife Alice
two pairs of flewes (herring nets) with their apparel and two

pairs of shot nets (mackerel nets), and his best silver spoon. His son John was to have two platters, dishes and saucers of pewter, and his second silver spoon. His daughters Joan, Agnes and Sybill each got a pewter dish, a candlestick and a silver spoon. And to his wife he left 2 acres on the Dyrlocks, his garden at Eastbrook and his house and close at William Joyes'.

A WEALTHY BURGESS

One more example which deserves notice is the will of Richard Reade, Mayor of Folkestone, dated 1578. He left personal effects to the total of £29 11s. 8d., including one silver goblet weighing eleven ounces, eight silver spoons weighing nine ounces, and four and a half ounces of 'old silver'. He had a large wardrobe valued at twenty-one pounds, including three 'gabours', two cloaks, two taffeta doublets and two fustian doublets, three cloth jerkins and a fur jerkin, and several pairs of gaskins. Among his bequests he gave 'to the poor people of Folkestone faggots of wood which were to be delivered every St. Thomas's day for the next twenty years following his death'. He bequeathed ten pounds to the town of Folkestone for the paving of the streets within the town where it was most needed. After various bequests to his relations he gave to his faithful servant, Wood, twenty 'lawful' pounds, a feather bed, a pair of blankets and three pairs of sheets. His niece, Olive Reade was bequeathed his silver service, and her sister Rebecca was to have his silver goblet. The will also disposes of the contents of his 'parlour, his kitchen, his hall, his chamber above the kitchen, and other'. Richard Reade must have had a fair-sized house, possibly on the Bayle, and well-furnished.

TUDOR HOUSE ON THE BAYLE

One such house of the Tudor period survived on the Bayle until 1916. Although at a later date it had been divided into two dwellings, it was evident when it was demolished that it was a well-built stone house with handsome Tudor fireplaces, pargetted ceilings and pannelled rooms. It was obviously the home of a well-to-do burgess who had prospered and could enjoy the amenities of the day. It is a pity it could not have been preserved.

THE PARISH CHURCH

The growing prosperity was reflected in the additions to the parish church. We must retrace our steps to the place where we left it in the last chapter. In 1095 Nigel de Muneville, as we saw, rebuilt the church after the depredations of Earl Godwin, and founded a new Priory for Benedictine monks in place of the old nunnery. It was built close to the site of the old nunnery, and some forty years later the monks became apprehensive about the state of the cliff which was slipping away. So at the monks' request the succeeding lord of the manor, William D'Averanches, built a new church and priory outside the boundaries of the castle (now called the Bayle), and slightly to the west of it. This was the foundation of the present parish church, dating from 1138. It was dedicated to St. Mary and St. Eanswythe, and presumably Eanswythe's relics were moved to this church. Not much of this building is now visible, but it it thought that the two-bay arcades of the chancel with their blocked circular clerestorey windows may date from this period. The bases of the piers are now below the level of the floor which has since been raised.

During the troubles when King John was in the district, the church was again sacked, as we said, by the French in 1216. Four years later, in 1220, it was restored, but so thoroughly that few features of the twelfth-century building remained. There was a considerable rebuilding and enlargement again in 1236 when Hamo de Crevequer succeeded to the barony. He extended the chancel farther east and inserted the three lancet windows with their triple shafts and the vesicle above. Altogether the new church in the Early English style must have made a striking impression, and it resembled the present Alkham Church which was built on the same plan. It had a small square tower separating the conventual part from the parish church (the nave), and the transepts. The chancel chapels, both being shorter than the chancel, as at Alkham, were rebuilt, the south chapel being substantially as it is now. But both were altered in the next century, that on the north side being much enlarged in 1474, and the south having new windows inserted in 1464. This was a sign of increasing prosperity in the town, which at the end of the fifteenth century culminated in the enlarging of the central tower to its present

height. It was done in the perpendicular style, the old tower
being completely encased in new stone. It was vaulted internally
and where the ribs met a circular bell-rope hole was made.
Stone seats were provided round the bases of the piers, and a
spiral stair-case led up to the roof turret. Outside, buttresses
supported the structure which was strengthened to carry the
bell-frame. By 1500 the Priory church must have looked worthy
of the barony of Folkestone, and the lords of the manor contributed generously to its improvement.

FRATERNITIES

There is evidence that the monks made a great show of
ceremonial whenever the Lord of the Manor and his family
attended the services. The wealthy family of the Poynings
favoured the monks and Philipot refers to a 'leiger book'
setting forth the entertainment which the family were to have
when they attended high mass. The townsfolk were not behind-
hand in making their contributions too, and as we have seen
from various wills and bequests in the fifteenth and sixteenth
centuries the church had several altars and images, and there
were several fraternities connected with it. A fraternity was a
religious gild or brotherhood, to which members contributed
as a sort of social welfare scheme. They were assured of assistance in sickness, a special place in the church and burial
benefits. We shall refer to these again when we discuss the
Guildhall. There were at least three fraternities—one called
'The Light of the Little Cross', another 'The Fraternity of the
Purification of St. Mary the Virgin' and another 'The Light of
the Corpus Christi'. Various members left money in their wills
to the fraternities, or for lights to be kept burning at the altars
and images. In 1458 Matthew Waryn left ten marks for new
vestments—the church is famous for its fine vestments—and in
1463 Alice Brette left a tablecloth and a basin to the Altar of
St. Mary of Pity; and in 1464 John Reade left five marks for a
new missal. In the same year the south chancel aisle was rebuilt
and decorated according to the will of John Baker.

THE ROOD BEAM

From John Reade's will we also learn that there was behind
the High Altar a beam which stretched across the Chancel,

and most likely carried a large Rood Cross. Behind this again there was a space dedicated to the Virgin, and we learn that in 1472 John Cole left 4d. to 'The Light of St. Mary behind the High Altar'. When we remember that the two aumbries in the present church are further from the east wall than is usual, we can assume that the High Altar was originally further forward than it is now, so as to allow for a Lady Chapel with an altar, shrine or image behind. All this decoration was carried out before the suppression of the Priory, so we may assume that wealthy parishioners had special access to the conventual church. In the second half of the fifteenth century bequests were made for the 'pewing' of the church, a fact which reminds us that before this parishioners normally stood by the various altars at Mass; but now townsfolk were beginning to think of their comfort and were wealthy enough to pay for it. In 1500 there were five chapels, five aisles and thirteen lights. The townsfolk now had a church of which they might well be proud.

CHAPTER FIVE

FOLKESTONE IN THE SIXTEENTH AND SEVENTEENTH CENTURIES

A T the beginning of the sixteenth century Folkestone was still a mere village in size, if we are to judge it by modern standards. But by contemporary standards it ranked as a 'town' with a Mayor and Corporation, possessing all the privileges that went with their Charter as a limb of the Cinque Ports. It had an official civic life of its own and its citizens jealously guarded their privileges and exercised their rights. It is owing to the fact that the Corporation had a Chamberlain who kept records of their transactions that we have a fair knowledge of the life of the times, although the records consist chiefly of money payments. Without these records our knowledge would be very slight. The population was still only about 700 and they were mostly illiterate, for there were as yet no schools and they had no use for learning. The citizens merely made their marks when they had to sign a document—a practice which lasted in Folkestone as in other places until the beginning of the nineteenth century.

THE CONSTITUTION

In 1545 the Corporation was enlarged by the addition of twenty-four Councillors. All the Jurats and Councillors were elected from the freemen of the town, and the appointment lasted for life. Local government was, therefore, self-perpetuating—an oligarchy in fact. But freemen could not refuse to serve, and were bound to accept the position of Jurat or Mayor if elected, on pain of severe penalty. Consequently we see the same names appearing again and again in the records. The freemen elected a Mayor annually who with the Bailiff, acted as Coroner and Judge; they also appointed two of their members to collect the town's rates and dues and for the payment of salaries and accounts. These officers were later reduced to one who was called the Chamberlain. He kept all

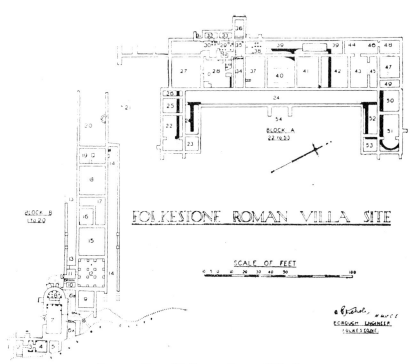

PLATE 1. Plan of Folkestone Roman Villa Site.

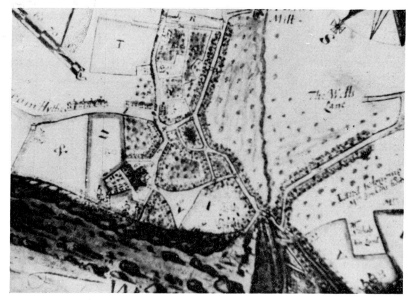

PLATE 2. Plan of Folkestone in 1697. From the survey made by Abraham Walter.
(By kind permission of the Earl of Radnor.)

PLATE 3. Folkestone from the sea, *c.* 1790. (Detail from an engraving in Hasted's *History of Kent.*)

PLATE 4. West Cliff and the Stade, *c.* 1785. (From a painting by William Marlow in Folkestone Museum.)

PLATE 5. Prior's Lees, the Parish Church and the harbour under construction in 1811. (Original watercolour.)

PLATE 6. This picture shows the accumulation of shingle behind the western pier, and the curious arrangement of the stones of the pier. Note the boatbuilder's shed on the site of the future Pavilion Hotel. (Watercolour in Folkestone Museum, *c.* 1820.)

PLATE 7. The completed harbour in 1823 as seen from the East Cliff. (From a lithograph by William Daniell.)

PLATE 8. The harbour in 1845 after its adoption by the South Eastern Railway. Note the S.E. Jetty, the Pavilion Hotel and the offices of the Harbour Board. (Watercolour by G. B. Campion.)

the accounts and records, and was in fact both Town Clerk and Treasurer. All the official business of the town was decided by the members of the Corporation who paid a fine of sixpence if they missed a Council meeting; but they received sixpence for recording their votes. The election of the Mayor every year was carried out with due ceremony at the Mayoral Cross in the Parish Churchyard, and it was followed by a banquet at the town's expense. Something of the spirit of the occasion may be glimpsed from this entry in the minutes for 1596:

'M^d. that uppon the viiith daie of September in the xxxviiith year of the reign of o^r soferan ladie Queene Elizabeth, being the feaste daie of the natyvitie of o^r ladie, Henry Philpott, maior, & the jurats and comons of this towne of ffolkestone, did at the sound of the comon horne assemble themselves together at the crosse in the churche yard of ffolkestone to elect a mayor for the yere to coome, accordinge to the ancient vsages, liberties, & fraunchises of the same towne time oute of minde vsed. And after the cause of the said assemblie notified to the said comons, the comon chest opened & the records therein openly shewed & the customals of the said towne distinctly read, the said comons departed into the churche to their election, and did elect Willyam Read, jurate, to be maior of the saide towne for the yere to coome, whoe theruppon took the oathe of the supremacie, & after the oathe for the office of mayraltye.'

After this the accounts show expenses for a public dinner, and charges made by the Wardens for blowing the town horn, for carrying the town chest and for beer, wine and bread.

In 1582 the Minutes make mention for the first time of the Common Council. It would appear to have been an innovation for the record states very fully that the Mayor, John Warde, gentleman, and Jurats of the town of Folkestone 'have elect and chosen by the consent of the whole commons, 25 commoners, in the name of the whole commonality, to be a town council to make and to agree unto all such necessary laws as shall be thought good by the Mayor and Jurats of the town of Folkestone . . .'; here follow twenty-five names including Richard Elwood, 'town clerk'. One wonders what the twenty-four Councillors had been doing since 1545.

DUTIES

The chief duties of the Corporation were (1) to carry out orders from the Lord Warden, such as special levies of taxes (called 'cesses') for ships or to repair the defences of the town; (2) to fit out and provision a certain number of boats for the mackerel fishing season off Yarmouth, to collect dues upon the fish brought ashore, and upon goods landed from trading ships; (3) to maintain a watch, to keep law and order, to try criminals and to punish them, and to settle disputes between citizens. They had the power of life and death over their fellows (see note in Appendix 2); (4) to regulate the conditions of trade, to ensure fair dealing by tradesmen, and to supervise markets and fairs and collect dues for 'occupying'; to admit suitable persons to become 'freemen' of the town, and to ensure that no 'foreigner' set up in business, on pain of a fine of six and eight-pence per day; (5) to see to the distribution of charities to the poor, and to keep paupers from others districts off the parish; (6) to keep accounts and records.

INCOME

The revenues of the town were not very great and it is estimated that the average income during the sixteenth century was about £60 a year. Sometimes it was much less. In 1516 it amounted to £14 10s. 4d.; and in 1597 the town's account was so low that the corporation had to borrow eleven pounds to pay the town's debts. The Mayor and several Jurats lent money until a general cess could be made to defray all charges. The town's income was derived, as we have indicated, from dues on fish, caught in the town boats, from hook-fare, dues on salt-fish, rents from traders for 'occupying', i.e. plying their trade from permitted premises; from a tax on slaughtered animals, and a duty on all goods brought into the town for sale; fines imposed by the Court, and fees charged for the admission of freemen to the Borough.

THE PRIORY

One event of considerable importance to the town took place in 1535 when the Priory was suppressed. It was one of the earliest to be closed and apparently it went without any dispute. It was the beginning of a long period of decline in the fortunes of the Parish church which contrasted with the great prosperity of the previous century. There was only the Prior and one sick monk in the place at the time, and it needed only

a little persuasion to get the Prior to resign. Philipot reported:
'It was so artfully managed by the King's Commissioners, that
many of the members of them were brought over to desire to
leave their possession and habit, and some of them gave up
their houses, among which was the Prior and Convent of
Folkestone, who signed their resignation on 15th November,
1535; Thomas Bassett (or Barrett) being the Prior of it, who
had a pension of ten pounds per annum.' The moribund
condition of the Priory may account for the increased activities
of the townsfolk in using and decorating the convent church,
as we have already seen. The parishioners also seem to have
been more actively concerned with poor relief, and we shall
refer to this when we consider the history of the old Guildhall.

PREPARATION FOR WAR

At this period Folkestone came into touch with our national
history. As a result of Henry VIII's break with Rome and the
establishment of the Church of England, there was considerable alarm from rumours of invasion from France. In 1538
the Pope ordered the Bull of Excommunication against Henry
to be put into force, and the King fully expected a French army
to cross the Channel. The coastal defences were strengthened,
and new castles were built at Sandown, Deal, Walmer, Sandgate and Camber. They were all built on a uniform plan with
a circular central tower, and flanking semi-circular turrets,
making a clover pattern. Deal Castle is the best surviving
example, but it was Sandgate Castle which affected the citizens
of Folkestone most. The complete accounts for the building
are still in existence, and they show that the total cost was
£2,884 14s. od. It took eighteen months to build, but bad weather
and three weeks' Christmas holidays accounted for three
months, so the whole took only fifteen months. The King's master-
mason was in charge of the work, and in one month no fewer
than 900 men were employed, either in building, or in carting
stone and timber. The work was obviously done under pressure
as the invasion was greatly feared. Most of the stone came from
local quarries, or from the recently dissolved monasteries
nearby. In fact, stone from Folkestone Priory, St. Radegund's
Abbey and Monk's Horton was used. The invasion never came
—possibly because we were so well prepared.

In Folkestone there was considerable preparation for the expected enemy. Trenches were dug, butts thrown up, and sites made for a gun or guns on the former Priory site. Bows and arrows were delivered and a quantity of gunpowder bought at 4d. or 5d. a pound. The guns had to be fetched from Cobham, where the Lord Warden of the Cinque Ports lived, and brought to the cliff site on the Bayle. Trenches and butts were also constructed on the East Cliff—by a labourer, William King, and it took him seven days with the assistance of Roger Jenkyn, the Piper. The loads of turf for the butts were carried by William Tybold, Thomas Baker, Jurat, and Mistress Baker. The matter was obviously urgent.

In the early forties Henry VIII felt confident enough to turn the tables on the French, and so preparations were made for the siege of Boulogne. Folkestone was required to send six or seven men fully equipped for the army, and the records show an entry headed 'Charges of six men over-sea soldiers'. They include:

In primis for 6 harnesses	£3
Item for 6 upper garments and 6 upper stocks of hosen, each of them 13/4, whereof paid	40/–
Item for making of 3 doublets	2/–
Item 6 pair of boots	14/–
Item 6 swords Item 6 daggers Item 2 sword girdles	18/–

The town was evidently proud of its little army, for 'Master Mayor and other company' escorted them to Dover. The journey (there and back) took them three days!

Meanwhile Henry was mustering his army at Dover in preparation for the invasion and looking for ways and means of transporting it across the Channel. Sir John Moynings, Lieutenant of Dover Castle, put a restriction on the local fishing and trading boats, and ordered a watch to be kept for Scots ships, as an alliance had been formed between Scotland and France to counteract Henry's plans. Any French ships sighted were to be captured and the French ports blockaded. On 4th August, 1543 a proclamation of war was made upon France, and local fishermen were allowed to go fishing once more.

PLANS FOR A HARBOUR

It was intended to use Folkestone as a port of embarkation for some of the troops and supplies, but there existed only a rudimentary pier or mole. This probably consisted of a mere bulwark of stone or timber to which a boat might be moored at high tide. Henry was interested enough to see if a plan could be formed for turning the place into an effective port. In 1541 he sent a certain Master Tuk and Master Captain of Sandgate to take a 'site' for a harbour. Master Tuk drew up a plan for which he was presented with a conger worth 20d. The plan was not adopted and so next year the King himself came down to Folkestone on Tuesday, 2nd May, 1542 to inspect the place, and returned to Dover on Saturday, 6th May. Meanwhile, on the Friday, four men, Richard Cavendish, John Bartlett, John Borow and Anthony Aucher had come to take a site for the harbour. These men had already made a new plan for Dover Harbour, a plan which still exists in the British Museum. But nothing came of the plan for Folkestone; however the town managed to despatch 220 men, 40 horses and 10 bullocks to France.

FESTIVITIES

The occasion of the King's visit was celebrated in the town with appropriate festivities; a barrel of beer was fetched from Ralph Wollets, the brewer, the Earl of Hertford's Minstrel's performed at Master Baker's, and the King's bearward brought a bear and a wolf for public entertainment. Bear baiting, minstrels and players were always welcome, and the town was often visited by troupes of strolling players who were maintained by the nobility. Within a period of nine years players and minstrels are mentioned ten times each and bearwards seven times. When the players and minstrels came they performed at Master Baker's or at Master Kenet's at the 'Cheker'. These performances would be given in the inn-yard or in the street in front of the Mayor's house. Both the King's and the Queen's Players appeared and those of the Lord Warden. We do not know what plays were performed except for one called 'Iope'; but on one occasion the Lord of Misrule visited the town. He was lord of the ceremonies (at the Christmas festivities, which lasted three weeks), and his expenses for beer, bread and wine when he performed at Folkestone and Sandgate, came to 7/6. Other entertainers who amused the people were the King's Jester, and a certain William the Lutor who played and sang. Life must have been a little less drab when these entertainers came to the town.

If we may look forward to the end of this century, we find that in the summer of 1597 Shakespeare's troupe made a tour through Sussex and Kent, visiting Rye in August, and acting in Dover on the 3rd September. The company would pass through Folkestone on their way from Rye, but there is no record to show that his players performed here. But Shakespeare must have climbed to the top of Aycliffe, as his description in King Lear of the samphire-gatherers on the cliff shows, and the cliff has been named after him ever since. His company performed again at New Romney in May, 1609, and in April, 1612, and possibly on other occasions. Other troupes also went on tour, but we have no further information about them.

QUEEN ELIZABETH'S VISIT

In 1573 Queen Elizabeth made a progress through Kent. She stayed at Westenhanger for a night and on resuming her journey to Dover she was met on Folkestone Down by the Mayor and Jurats who presented their compliments to her. But they were somewhat eclipsed by the arrival of the Archbishop of Canterbury, the Lord Cobham and a huge number of knights who accompanied her to Dover where she stayed a week. In 1587 Elizabeth came again, this time to see that the coastal defences were sound, and also to see whether the Cinque Ports really deserved their special privileges. She announced 'she did not meane to suffer them in such fruitless manner to enjoye so great privileges without doing any service, but to resume them into Her Majestie's hands and to reduce them to the same terms that the rest of her subjects bordering upon the sea coast are in'. She was in no favourable mood when she came, but perhaps she thought it wiser, in view of the national emergency, to do nothing about curtailing the privileges of the Cinque Ports.

THE SPANISH WAR

The national emergency was, of course, the threatened invasion by the Spanish Armada, and preparations to resist the enemy were made once more. Folkestone sailors were interrogated for information about Spanish ships; in addition to the usual contribution of ships to Dover, a special cess was made for the 'setting forthe of a ship in warlike sort, according to an order taken by Mr. Levetenant, by the aucthorytye of the lord treasurer and other lords of her majesty's privy counsell'. The government was constantly issuing orders for the recruitment and training of the county militia, and Folkestone was required to train 135 men as her contribution. She probably sent far fewer since the town was already supplying sailors and boats. However, recruiting and drilling went on, more guns were mounted on the cliffs and kept in readiness. Selected soldiers were sent on special service to Dover, or to drill there, and the Lieutenant of Dover Castle made repeated inspections of the town's defences.

Even after the defeat of the Armada in 1588, Folkestone made a generous contribution to the war overseas. On 9th February, 1596, another cess was made by the Mayor and Jurats 'as well on oute men's lands and goods as home men's, for and towards the setting forthe of shipping in that great viag to Cadiz in Spaine, under the conduct of the most valiant chieftain, the Lord of Essex, his honour and the right honourable Lord High Admiral of England . . .' The Earl himself seems to have visited the town (and perhaps this accounts for their generosity), but the only reference to it in the accounts is the following: 'Item, paide for a lantern, lost when the Earl of Essex passed through the town, 12d.' It was in the following year that the Council had to borrow money from the Mayor to pay its debts.

THE WATCH

Again and again in this century the town's defences were repaired and the watch was re-organized from time to time. In 1599 for example the town issued a special order concerning the watch:

'Moved that the 13th day of August, in the 41st year of her Majesty's reign, it was by William Jynkin, maior, Thomas Harvy, Henry Philpot . . . and several others, juratts, uppon iminent daunger of the enemy his landing within this land, ordered that presently a watch for this town should be sett nightly in form following: viz., 2 at Harborough, 2 at the

stade, and 2 at Priors lease, and 2 and 2 within the town, and
that the householders themselves shall watch (if they be men
fytt) untill further orders; and that the watch shall begin at the
ringing of the bell about 7 of the clock at night, and leave of
betweene 5 and 6, at the ringing of the bell in the morning;
and that the watch shall be serched by 2 horsemen . . . and it
is also ordered that all persons inhabityng within this town shall
repaire to the place of randevowe in the towne uppon the
ringing of the great bell, if they shall be within the hearth of
the same uppon paine to be punished at the discretion of the
maior and juratts.'

These were stringent measures for the time, and are strongly
reminiscent of firewatching in the last war.

WELFARE

Now let us consider another aspect of life in the town—the
treatment of the poor and needy. Apart from pestilence and
common accidents, fishing families were always liable to suffer
the loss of the breadwinner at sea, with consequent hardship
to the widows and children. Before the dissolution of the
Priory in 1535 poor relief was given by the clergy or the monks,
but this source dried up with the loss of the Priory. Perhaps it
was on account of this that a fair number of charities were
instituted by well-to-do citizens for the benefit of the poor. In
the period from 1480 to 1660 they came to a total value of £367,
not counting £200 which was earmarked by the Harvey family
for special purposes. This was a large sum for a town of the size
of Folkestone. The benefactions often took the form of clothing,
bread, coal and faggots, and the charities were usually vested in
the Mayor and Jurats, who were required to distribute the
gifts. After the disappearance of the Priory a place had to be
found for the distribution—often called a 'livery dole'. The
obvious place was the Guildhall, which was situated near the
church at the end of Mercery Lane (our Church Street) where it
joined Butcher Row (our Rendezvous Street).

ORIGIN OF THE GUILDHALL

There is something of a mystery about the old Guildhall since
there is no record to show who built it or when it was built.
It is curious, too, that the town should have a Guildhall, but no

trade or craft guilds. In his account of the Cinque Ports, Harris throws a little light on the question. He says:

> 'The Ports have also the Privilege of being a Gild, or as it was afterwards written, a Guild; that is, a Fraternity, Society, or Community of Men, who gelded or paid all common Charges out of a common Stock; and had beside, all the Franchises of a Court-Leet, and Court Baron. The Members of such a Gild, or Company, are often in our old Books called Gildones, and Congildones; and they used to hold their Gilden, or public Feasts, in some great Room or Hall, which hence was called the Guild Hall . . .'

This seems to suit our old Guildhall very well; and a further suggestion can be found in M. Burrows's book, *The Cinque Ports*. He notes that there is an entry in Domesday Book for Dover of the 'Gihalla of the burgesses'. This is an early reference; but during the following centuries Merchant Guilds became a prominent feature of several towns, which, owing to the increase of trade, were growing in importance, especially in the twelfth and thirteenth centuries. Burrows notes that the Cinque Ports were exceptions to the general rule. 'None of them possessed a Merchant Guild, although one would fully expect them to have one. In the case of the Ports their ancient institutions took its place. Their franchises of imposing and assessing taxes for the whole Confederation, of holding Courts . . . supplied a substitute for the guild-merchant in separate towns, and was of itself a guild of a larger kind. The term "guildhall" was indeed used for "townhall" in some of the Ports, but it has been a comparatively modern use, connected probably with modern guilds of the sixteenth century, and especially in the time of Queen Elizabeth.' This suggestion would certainly serve to explain the origin of our Guildhall, particularly as the increase in market days testifies to the growing trade of the town; and with the grant of a Charter in 1313 the need for a guildhall in which to transact town business would be all the more urgent. It would also be a welcome rendezvous for the members of the fraternities where they could hold their feasts and dispense their charity. When we remember the pomp and ceremony of the Mayor-making days it is hard to believe that they did not have their ceremonials too; but it must be admitted that we have no direct evidence of them.

DESCRIPTION OF THE OLD GUILDHALL

It must have been a very early building as it needed considerable repair in the middle of the sixteenth century. In 1565 the town paid for extensive repairs to the building. A whole page of the accounts is given over to items which amount to many pounds, including entries for lime, bricks, tiles, lattices and paint for the hall. 'Paid in expense upon the painter coming to town to take the Town Hall to paint, 6d.; paid to the painter for painting the Town Hall, 20s.; paid for three faggots for the painter to heat his colours, 3d.' From this time the place is referred to as the Town Hall—thus in 1607, 'Item, paid to the glazier for the Town Hall windows.' (This was the first time glass was used for the Hall.) Yet in February, 1616, it is again referred to as the 'Guildhall', showing that the old name persisted, and in fact remained in use until the nineteenth century. The old building, much repaired in 1616 and in 1730, lasted until 1840 when it was demolished. No drawing of it is now in existence, but both Mackie and Stock describe it in mock affectionate terms:

'The old Guildhall was a four-sided gabled affair, of a shape that was neither a square nor a parallelogram, none of the four sides being of like dimensions, with an angle projecting over the corner of the street, from whence a narrow staircase led up a flight of steps into the hall itself, which, after the erection of a new one, was for a long time used as an office by the town clerk. Its demolition took place in 1840. Its age must have been considerable, for in the reign of Henry VIII there are repeated entries for repairs such as are not likely to have been required in a new structure; and its dilapidation was so great in 1730 that it was found necessary to support it with shores. Beneath the Hall was a small market, in the corner of which was a dirty dark cell, used as a lock-up, and appropriately termed the Black Hole.' And Stock adds 'a place of terror to all the urchins of the town.'

The odd shape of the Guildhall was due to the fact that it stood on an acute angle at the junction between two streets; and it was situated much further forward than the present junction, since Butcher Row was as narrow as High Street is now. It was to this building that the poor came to receive charity, and all the official business of the town was conducted in it. The church was playing a less prominent part in the life of the town, as from 1566 onwards the vicar was replaced by a curate, and for certain periods there was no incumbent at all; consequently more social work fell to the Corporation officials.

SCHOOLING

As for the 'urchins of the town' as Stock calls them, there was no regular school for them to go to in Folkestone. The first mention of a schoolmaster appears in the records in 1564. 'Paid to John Corke's wife for the board of the schoolmaster that came to the town at Christmas to tech children, 5s. 2d.' This was probably a travelling scrivener who would spend a month or two at each place he visited. In Tudor times a schoolmaster needed the formal licence of the Bishop before he was allowed to teach. The local churchwardens were not very particular about this. In 1581 they did not know whether a man named Johnson 'schoolmaster in our parish hath a licence or no'; in 1602 Mr. Fludd taught in the chancel of the parish church 'being not licensed to our knowledge'; in 1603 Richard Barker taught in school although unlicenced, 'and even read prayers openly in our church upon divers Sundays and other Holy days not being licensed there-unto, nor within orders as far as we know'. Schooling seems to have been scant and unorthodox, but there was a system of apprenticeship in the town which was important since the freemen of the town were often recruited from apprentices who had completed their indentures. The Statute of Artificers of 1563 enacted that every craftsman in town or country had for seven years to learn his craft under a master who was responsible for him. As G. M. Trevelyan points out it was the very practical answer made by our ancestors to the ever-present problems of technical education and the difficult 'after-school age'. In the records, for instance, we find that John Elgar served a seven years' apprenticeship to his father, a builder and carpenter. Girls too were apprenticed, for we learn that Alice Stills, apprenticed in 1618 to Solomon Harvie was whipped for running away. Apart from this kind of practical education there was little opportunity for general training or learning to read and write, and probably fishermen's sons got less than any.

THE FREE SCHOOL

It was with these poor fisher boys in mind that Dr. William
Harvey, his brother Eliab and his nephew Sir Eliab Harvey
founded between them the free school we now know as the
Harvey Grammar School. In his will Dr. William Harvey left
£200 to the Mayor of Folkestone for the use of the poor of the
town. Although the founding of a school was not mentioned in
the will, it is likely that William had discussed the possibility
with Eliab before his death, but had left the matter open. Both
were local boys and had had to go away to school; William went
to King's School, Canterbury, and was probably aware of the
serious lack of education in Folkestone. In the year following
Dr. Harvey's death Eliab invested William's legacy in a small
farm called Combe Farm, near Lympne, the rent of which was
to supply the endowment of the school. The fact that Eliab
acted so promptly after his brother's death suggests that
William had intended it to be done. Unfortunately Eliab
himself died in 1661 before he could complete the task, and it
fell to his son, Sir Eliab, to execute both his father's and his
uncle's wills. In 1671 he purchased the site of the future school
in Rendezvous Street, and in 1674 he executed the Foundation
Deed of the Free School for 20 poor boys to be taught to read
and write English, and if desired, Latin. Out of the endowment
the master's salary was to be paid, fishing boats to be provided
as necessary, and the Tanlade to be kept in repair. So at last
in 1674 Folkestone got its first school, known as a Free School
to begin with, and later the Grammar School. And local boys
who showed an aptitude for study could learn to read and write,
and, if they wished, learn Latin and go to University as Dr.
William Harvey himself had done.

THE HARVEYS

The Harvey family was a remarkable one in many ways,
and they provide an interesting example of what might be
done by enterprising men in the late Tudor period. Thomas
Harvey (father of William), inherited a little farm, called
Dane Farm, just behind the Crete Road West, and he married
Juliana Jenkin of Hastingleigh. She died in childbirth, so
Thomas married again, this time Joan Halke of Canterbury.
Both of his fathers-in-law had carriers' businesses, and Thomas

joined forces with them, exporting wool and importing continental products through the port of Folkestone. He must have abandoned farming as his main interest for according to tradition, he set up in business in Folkestone, in Mercery Lane opposite the Guildhall. His second wife brought him a large family including seven sons. The eldest, Dr. William Harvey took to medicine, but all the others joined their father in establishing a Turkey Merchant business and in money lending, Thomas was Mayor of Folkestone four times, the last time in 1611, but after 1605 when his wife Joan died, his interest turned to London where his sons were developing the family firm. They all grew incredibly rich and were able to buy country houses and become members of the landed gentry. No doubt Folkestone was a conveniently obscure place to import contraband goods, and once or twice the Harveys were required to appear before the Privy Council to pay the evaded duties. They were wealthy enough, however, to avoid trouble and their cases were dropped. But they did not forget their native town, for we find that in 1636 Dr. William Harvey and his brothers presented a petition to Charles I asking that certain lands formerly belonging to Folkestone Priory should be granted on lease for the benefit of the town. The petition was granted. Dr. William was Physician in Ordinary to the King and on friendly terms with him, and this no doubt helped. In all their dealings education and enterprise stood them in good stead, qualities noticeably lacking in Folkestone at that time.

THE FISHERMEN

Most of the population were content to carry on with their fishing and trading, and seek their fortunes and adventures on the element they knew best. But it was a lawless age on the sea, and sea-farers had to be prepared to resist piratical attacks from any quarter. The French, the Dutch, the Spaniards and the Scots were always potential enemies according to the state of contemporary politics. In February, 1616, a special cess was levied 'to be contributed toward the setting fforth of shipps to suppresse the pyrates of Algeers and Tunes . . .' The fishermen, and the townsfolk as well, were always liable to meet unexpected taxes of this kind, and it often became a burden. On this occasion 40 marks had to be found.

The fishermen complained as far back as 1592 that they could not afford the dues exacted by the Corporation upon the fish caught, amounting to one half the value of the catch. Accordingly the Corporation enacted that 'all fishermen of the town shall be discharged yearly for ever hereafter of and for the payment of the said half-share of and upon every of their fishing seasons to the Chamber'. Instead of the half share a toll of one penny on every pound's worth of fish brought in, whether 'herring fare, shot fare, or Scarborough season', was imposed, and for every wand of fish, sixpence. The fishermen were required to buy in the town, all the victuals for their voyages, on pain of a fine of five shillings, a very large sum. At the end of the seventeenth century there was a noticeable scarcity of fish, and so restrictions were placed upon the use of boats for trawling. It was forbidden to trawl before the 12th March and then only on four specified days of the week—Mondays, Tuesdays, Thursdays and Fridays: penalty 20s.

The catching of fish in kettle nets was common practice, and it was sometimes a temptation to unscrupulous men. One man, Adrian Godden, 'for privie pycking and taking of fish out of Richard Minter's kiddolle nett', was kept in custody until nine next morning and then put in the stocks for three hours—'a wryting of pyckerye to be sett on his head showing the cause of punishmt'. Justice was summary and public in those days.

The tale of taxation went on through the century. In 1634 the Cinque Ports were required to provide a large vessel of 800 tons for the fleet, and Folkestone had to provide its share. A 'special cess' was raised 'by virtue of a writ directed from his Majesty' and everyone had to pay up, some of the poorer citizens providing as little as 3d. The total subscribed was £35 10s. 6d. This was the beginning of the Ship Money dispute, and no doubt Folkestone men felt the effect of it in their pockets.

THE CIVIL WAR

Fortunately the disturbances of the Civil War and the Commonwealth made little difference to the life of the town. Probably its remoteness from the main currents of national communication protected it from undue distress. Its sympathies were vaguely royalist, but since the County sided with Parliament, it was thought politic to follow suit. As a limb of Dover, Folkestone received its official instructions from Dover Castle; it was important for the Parliamentarians to secure Dover Castle as the chief stronghold of the county. It was captured on the night of 21st August, 1642, by a dozen townsmen, who scaled the walls, surprised the guard and got possession of the Castle. The garrison at the time consisted of only twenty men, who put up no resistance. It is thought that the governor, Sir Edward Boys, connived at the capture and made it easy; in any case, he was serving shortly afterwards on a Parliamentarian County Committee. The effect on Folkestone was mainly to force the resignation of Royalist sympathisers from the town council, and their places were taken by Parliamentarians. There must have been a considerable amount of argument among opposing parties in the town, if we may judge from the increased number of recognisances to keep the peace. Furthermore, the application of the puritanical act against swearing of 1651 cost Folkestone fishermen a heavy amount in fines for improper language. At the Restoration in 1660, by order from Dover, the Commonwealth Jurats were replaced by Royalist sympathizers, and that was that.

One matter which troubled the serious minded citizens was the lack of a suitable priest at the Parish church. For many years the parishioners had had to be content with a curate, often shared with another church. There were whole periods when there was no ordained priest to solemnize marriages, christenings or even funerals, some of the services being taken by the mayor. Part of the difficulty was that the Archbishop who held the appointment of the living, let it out at a reduced stipend to a curate instead of appointing a vicar. In 1641 Folkestone had an elderly minister, Peter Rogers, but he was so infirm and underpaid that the inhabitants sent a petition to Parliament asking for him to be pensioned off, and a new vicar installed. The terms of the petition reveal something of the state of affairs:

'That whereas Folkeston being a maior town, and a large parish extending itselfe two miles into the shire, the parsonage whereof, being an impropriation, and belonging to the Sea of Canterburie, the Lords of Canterburie still leasing out the same, and reserving to themselves 8o*l*. per annum, and a renewing fine everie fourth yeare, the tennant whereof now is Mr. Arnald Brames, who hath yett to come eleven yeares in itt, and letteth out the same for 300*l*. by the yeare; and yett the Lord of Canterburie doth allow his Curate of Folkeston but the bare stipend of 2o*l*. per annum, without having a house to live in, or any other help whatsoever. Now your petitioners doe humblie pray, that you would be pleased to grant such a competent allowance for the maintenance of the Minister of Folkeston, as in your wisdomes and pious care shalbe thought requisite; and whereas the Curate of Folkeston that now is, is a sicklie aged man and faileth much in his voice and sight, whereby he is not soe able to performe his ministeriall dutie as he himselfe would, and the parish requireth, your Petitioners doe further pray, that they may have a younger and a more pregnant man, for the performing of holie and divine service, and yett the old minister now being, may have some exhibition to keepe him during his life, and afterward the same to revert to the minister of Folkestone again.'

How much this petition tells us about the conditions of the the church at the time; and how good to see that the Folkestone Parishioners were more charitable than the Lords of Canterbury. But this was the beginning of a decline in church affairs which lasted for over a century.

THE HARBOUR

Another important question of the day, which was to occupy the town for the next 200 years, was the condition of the harbour. Henry VIII's plans, as we saw, came to nothing. In the next century the Stade, which had been protected hitherto by the headlands to some extent, became more and more exposed to the sea, and in rough weather banks of shingle and even houses would be washed away. At other times the shingle would be piled up, making it hard for the fishermen to draw their boats up out of harm's way. So in 1635 the Corporation ordered that 'on the beat of a drum at the command of the Mayor, every householder, or some fit and able person in his stead, should repair to the said harbour, each of them provided with shovels and other tools for clearing, scouring and expulsing the beach out of the said haven or harbour'. Defaulters were to be fined 6d. for every occasion they failed to turn out.

PLATE 9. The S.E. Jetty (Branch Line) and the first Swing Bridge, *c.* 1850. (From an engraving by J. F. Burrell.)

PLATE 10. Early Steam Packet leaving the Harbour. (From an engraving by G. R. Andrews.)

PLATE II. Folkestone Harbour, *c.* 1860. A very early photograph showing the Pavilion Hotel in the foreground, the Swing Bridge and three steam packets at the south quay. On the right are the Clock Tower, the Terminal Station and the Custom House. (Folkestone Museum.)

PLATE 12. The New Pier, *c.* 1876, showing the old groyne and the girder structure of the pier. The boat is probably the 'Victoria'. (Folkestone Museum.)

PLATE 13. Swedish cargo boat approaching the Horn Lighthouse. There was a great increase of goods traffic during the century. (Folkestone Museum.)

PLATE 14. The Clock Tower of the Harbour Offices and the early Pavilion Hotel. (Folkestone Museum.)

PLATE 15. The Viaduct and the Bradstone Mill, 1844. On the right is a farm, behind it the town windmill and in the centre the Rope Walks and Stace's house. On the left is the Bulldog Lane leading past Bradstone Mill. (Old engraving.)

PLATE 16. The same scene about 1860, a few years before Bradstone Road and Foord Lane were opened. (Folkestone Museum.)

This order implies that an attempt had been made to construct some sort of haven at the beginning of the century, but we have no information about it.

On 10th July, 1654, another order was issued by the Corporation—more urgent still:

> 'Whereas, heretofore, by the helpe and charge of divers well affected persons to this towne, and espetiallie of the right worshipful sir Bazil Dixwell, knight and baronett, deceased, late lord of the manor of this towne, the heades nowe standing and remayning by the seaside were made and erected with an intent to have a harbour for boates and shippes in the same place: and that after the same heades were so made, it fell out that the work could not take effect, yet notwithstanding, the said heades, by daylie experience, it is found, are very usefull and helpfull to preserve the stade of the said towne: and that of late time divers persons, not well considering the use and benefitt of them, have taken away many stones, rockes and other materials from the same, which in time of necessity must inevitablie be the overthrow of the said stade . . .'

The upshot was that persons convicted of damaging the works were to be fined ten shillings for each offence. From this we gather that considerable expense and trouble had been put into the building of jetties and moles (or 'heads' and 'knocks' as they called them); and that Sir Basil Dixwell had done much to help them, as his successors were to do later on. There was evidently a plan to construct a haven of some size, but it had never been completed. The elements were too strong for the resources of the day to combat them, and so we find on 12th February, 1699, at the very end of the century, another order stating that 'the "peere heads" of the late decayed harbour of this towne are very much ruined by rough tydes and great tempests' and that therefore all the able-bodied inhabitants must turn out to get rocks from the quarries and convey them to the harbour to mend the piers.

THE BOUVERIE FAMILY

And so the distressful tale went on, to be continued through the next century and a half. But before the end of the seventeenth century an event occurred which was to have considerable influence in the future. This was the purchase in 1697 of the Barony of Folkestone by Jacob des Bouverie, Esq., who was descended from a family of Turkey merchants of London. The new Lord of the Manor instructed his agent to make detailed plans and drawings of his estates, and these are still preserved in the Manor Office. They give a good picture of the town and district at the time they were made in 1697. In fact they provide us with the first map of the town.

THE TOWN IN 1700

The town fell into two parts: on the east was the Stade with the fishermen's dwellings clustered behind, a collection of houses lining the banks of the Pent stream, and a street of houses climbing up the old Dover lane. On the west side of the stream was a little alley called Gulston Street (later South Street), and another narrow street (High Street) climbing steeply up the hill to the Bayle, and bending round to Rendezvous Street. There were houses on three sides of the Bayle leaving the Bayle Pond and the Fair Place free. Beyond the pond was the Battery. Another short and narrow street called Butcher Row led from the Rose Inn in Rendezvous Street up the hill to Mercery Lane (Church Street), and a still narrower one, George Lane, joined High Street to Butcher Row. The latter curved round to connect with Shellons Lane, then only a cart track, but later to become Guildhall Street. There were a few houses at the bottom of Cow Lane (our modern Sandgate Road), and so called because it led to the place where a cattle fair was held. All beyond was farmland, and even the lower part of the Pent Valley where Tontine Street now is, was devoted to pasture and orchard gardens. The stream was liable to flood and so a small track led along the west side from High Street to Mill Lane where the Bradstone Mill was. It was called Mill Bay. The town can hardly have changed for a century, and there was to be little development for another century and a half.

CHAPTER SIX

EIGHTEENTH AND EARLY NINETEENTH CENTURY FOLKESTONE

THE eighteenth century saw a growing interest in history and several histories of Kent were produced at this time. Harris's *History of Kent* (1719) was never completed, but it gives 'an exact Topography or Description of the County', and with its maps and plates is an important volume. There is a fairly long account of Folkestone which set a pattern for many succeeding histories, but it is mainly concerned with the various noble families who owned the manor, and says little about the town. Seymour's *Survey of the Cities, Towns, and Villages of the County of Kent* (1776) is a little more informative. Hasted's *History of Kent* (1798) gives the fullest account of the landowners and their families but adds little information about the town or its inhabitants. Seymour is the most successful in presenting a picture of the place, and we quote a part of it:

> 'The town, in its present condition, is wealthy and populous; the streets are steep and narrow, and the irregularity of the buildings up and down the hills has something romantic, particularly the Church, in a point of land close to the sea. There are some neat houses facing the Church-yard, which have the advantage of a fine prospect. . . . A fine spring runs through the town, which is noted for the multitude of fishing boats that belong to its harbour. They are employed in the season in catching mackerel for London, to which they are carried by the boats of London and Barking. . . . In going from this town to Dover, the traveller meets with six or seven very romantic miles . . .'

Seymour presents a rather flattering picture; his statement that the town was wealthy is not borne out by the facts, as we shall discover later. The harbour was virtually non-existent; and the 'multitude of boats' might impress a landsman from Canterbury, but in fact the fishing had declined.

We get another glimpse of the town from William Gostling, who, in his *Walk in and about the City of Canterbury* (1774), says:

'Folkestone is a considerable fishing town, of such a hilly situation that it is hardly safe to ride in some of the streets of it. Being on the strand there some years ago, a pretty large vessel or two lay on the shore near me, and on asking some questions about them, I found they were their large mackarel boats, that the number belonging to the town was thirty two, which carried from fourteen to sixteen score of netting each.' (p. 198).

It would appear from Gostling's account that there were thirty-two large mackerel boats; he probably means that there were thirty-two boats of all kinds, only a few being used in mackerel fishing. Hasted writing in 1798 reports that there were eight or ten luggers or cutters employed in the mackerel fisheries, besides about thirty small boats for local fishing. 'They do not employ more than between two and three hundred men and boys,—who are under no regulation as a company.' This does not suggest a very large or well-organized fishing community.

OWLING AND SMUGGLING

In fact fishing as an employment had a growing rival in smuggling, as Defoe noted in his *Tour through the Whole Island of Great Britain* (1724).

'As I rode along this coast, I perceived several dragoons riding; officers, and others armed and on horseback, riding always about as if they were huntsmen, beating up their game; upon enquiry I found their diligence was employed in quest of the owlers, as they call them, and sometimes they catch some of them; but when I came to enquire further, I found too, that often times these are attacked in the night, with such numbers, that they dare not resist, or if they do, they are wounded and beaten, and sometimes killed; and at other times are obliged, as it were, to stand still, and see the wool carried off before their faces, not daring to meddle. But I find so many of these desperate fellows are of late taken up, by the courage and vigilance of the soldiers, that the knots are very much broken and the owling-trade much abated . . .'

Defoe was optimistic, or perhaps persuaded by the officers that the owling-trade was soon to be stamped out. In fact it was to go on throughout the century, but at this period (1725), the illicit export of wool was very profitable; and later on when the demand for wool declined the smuggling of contraband goods from the continent took its place and became an alternative source of income, not only to the seamen, but to many respectable and wealthy citizens inland who were behind the organized runs, and kept a conspiracy of silence about it. An entry in the records of Preventive Officers stated: 'As most of the inhabitants of Folkestone, Sandgate and Hythe are in the confidence of the smugglers, no information can be expected of them.' Of course contraband goods were brought in to the country on a large scale; spirits, tea, tobacco, silk, lace and other luxury goods. A certain Captain Cockburn gave evidence before a Royal Commission in 1746, and stated that at least six tons of tea and 2,000 half-ankers of brandy were imported every week from Boulogne. Another smuggler, Robert Hanning, testified that he had sold tea, brandies and wine to the value of £40,000 a year. Throughout this century and well into the next smuggling was a large and well-organized business, carried on all round the south-east coast; and Folkestone acquired a national reputation as a hotbed of smuggling. Coastguards and preventive officers were stationed along the coast, dragoons brought in to enforce the law, but it still went on unabated. In 1777 an Act was passed inflicting heavy penalties upon suspicious persons loitering within five miles of the coast. A coastal blockade was instituted in 1819, and eventually a brig, called 'The Pelter' was stationed in the Warren as a headquarters for Preventive Officers. The gangs of smugglers grew in size and influence, and sometimes bloody battles were fought in dark lanes and on lonely beaches.

There were losses: ships and their crews disappeared without trace, to the distress of their wives and children. Within a single period of two years four smuggling vessels which sailed from Folkestone were never heard of again. No less than thirty-two women became widows, and 146 children fatherless in consequence, and were dependent on the parish. When the cutter 'Jane' was lost with all hands at sea in 1823, the son of the captain said,

> 'Six of us were made orphans, the eldest 16 and the youngest a babe in arms. You can imagine the blow to my poor mother. We were left to live on the bounty of the people, and I must say we never wanted help.'

Folkestone men were sometimes caught and sentenced to transportation or compulsory service in the Navy. In May,

1820, eleven Folkestone men were held in Dover gaol, but a mob from Folkestone broke the gaol open and rescued them; they were never retaken. In January, 1823, Folkestone men were involved in a still more notorious case. The 'Four Brothers', a ship laden with £10,000 worth of contraband goods, set sail from Flushing with twenty-six seamen on board. She was intercepted by the preventive cutter, the 'Badger', some eight miles off Dungeness, and a gun-battle ensued. Four of the smugglers were killed and six injured, and one of the preventive officers was killed. The smugglers were induced to surrender by a trick and were taken prisoners. The men were tried at the Old Bailey, and the trial became something of a *cause célèbre*. Their friends feared that they would be hanged for murder, but they were tried for firing on a King's ship. They were acquitted on the grounds that the ship was Dutch and that more than half the men were of Dutch nationality. Actually they were mostly Folkestone men who had been born in Holland, so as to escape liability for pressed service in the navy. It was a not uncommon practice for pregnant women in Folkestone, if their husbands were seamen, to have their babies in Holland, and so protect their children from the press-gang. When the news of the acquittal reached Folkestone there was great jubilation, and the men were welcomed home like heroes.

GUINEA SMUGGLING

Another very remarkable kind of smuggling developed during the Napoleonic wars. It was necessary for the British forces in the Peninsula war to be supplied with money to carry on their campaigns under Wellesley. It was not possible to send the money openly by sea because of the naval blockade. It had to be done under cover, and Folkestone was a port sufficiently obscure for the purpose. The London Branch of the banking firm of Rothschild was commissioned to send golden guineas in specially built six-oared cutters, which were rowed across the channel to Dunkirk, where the French Branch of Rothschild's received them and passed them on to Portugal. Strangely enough, Napoleon knew all about this, but could do little; moreover, he hoped that Britain would soon be drained of its gold reserves, and so face economic collapse. The guineas were carried in long leather bags fitting the body, and the Folkestone crews, carefully selected and well paid, often carried as much as £30,000 in one crossing. A certain amount of secrecy had to be observed, and the journeys were always made at night; and there were always the preventive men to be avoided. Rothschild's had an agent in Folkestone, and it was his task to organize the crossings—sometimes under difficulties. The guineas were deposited in small lots among a number of reliable 'friends', and then quickly assembled for the transportation. Sometimes suspicion was aroused and matters had to be adjusted. The following episode, from a reliable source, illustrates this:

> 'The father and mother of the narrator lived in one of the narrow streets of old Folkestone, famous as a haunt of smugglers. The couple were about to retire to rest one dark and stormy night, when they were startled by a particular tapping at the window. Opening the door, the occupant of the house perceived a man enveloped in a huge cloak, and wearing a big slouch hat, which prevented his face from being seen. Motioning to him to keep silence, the stranger entered, and threw off his hat and cloak. He was the head of a very great financial firm, whose name is known all over the world. The old Folkestoner knew his visitor well. A few moments sufficed to explain how matters stood. The eminent financier had a trifling matter of a hundred thousand guineas, which he wanted to get safely across the Strait, and he wanted to secrete the sum till a favourable opportunity occurred. After much debating it was agreed at last that the couple should "sleep upon it" literally.
> 'Accordingly the gold was carefully brought in, in bags of a thousand guineas each. This was laid between the bed and the mattress—a hundred bags of shining gold! The couple slept on this, or, at least, tried to do, for the old boy afterwards declared that he spent the very uneasiest night of his life on that gold. Next day every bag was taken away . . .'

The Folkestone seamen knew that fortunes were being made from their efforts, and from the fact that the comparative obscurity of the port enabled transactions to be made away from public knowledge. It has been reported that a pigeon post was used to send secret and important news to financiers and merchants in London. Rothschilds had a supply of runners with relays of post-horses to take messages to their headquarters. News of battles won and lost in the Napoleonic wars had alarming effects on the Stock Exchange, and it behoved the large financiers to have the latest news as early as possible.

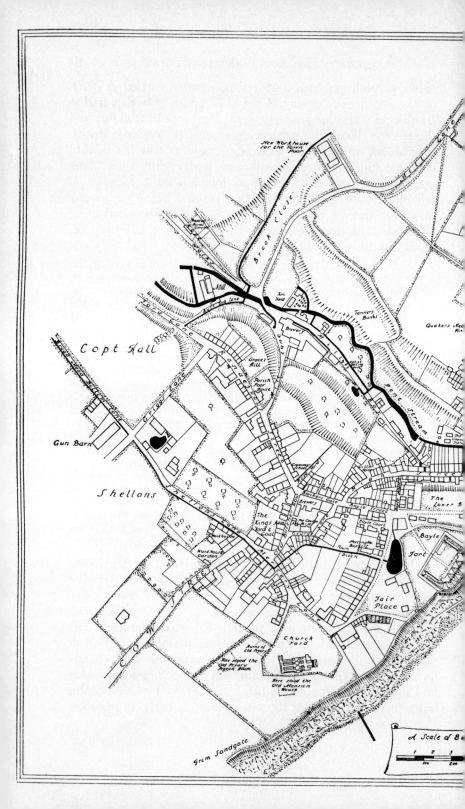

New Workhouse for the Town Poor

Brook Close

Copt Hall

Mill

Lane

Tan Yard

Brewery

Tanners Banks

Quakers Meeting

Grace's Mill

Penk Stream

Parish Poor House

Baptist Meeting

Gun Barn

Shellons

The Kings Arms Yard & Goal

Workhouse

Workhouse Garden

The

George

Bayle Court

The Lower B

Bayle

Fort

Fair Place

Church Yard

Ruins of Old Priory

Here stood the Old Priory Pigeon House

Here stood the Old Mansion House

Green Sandgate

A Scale of 8

1 2 3

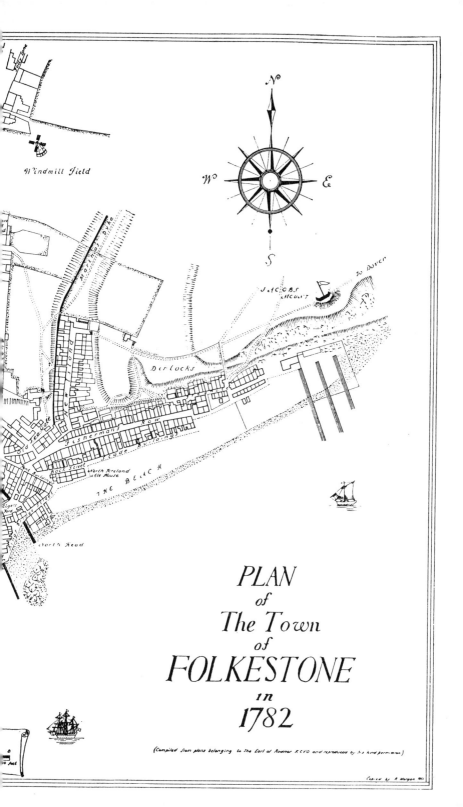

Windmill Field

N

W   E

S

MOYLAN DYKE

To Dover

JACOBS MOUNT

Dorlocks

Fishermans Road

Rock Street

North Foreland
Castle House

THE BEACH

North Head

PLAN
of
The Town
of
FOLKESTONE
in
1782

(Compiled from plans belonging to the Earl of Radnor K.C.V.O. and reproduced by his kind permission)

Copied by R Morgan 1951

When the result of the Battle of Waterloo was still awaited in England, Nathan Rothschild himself stood on the pier at Folkestone, and was handed by his agent the printed report in a Dutch newspaper twelve hours before anyone knew the result in England. He immediately raced off to London, sold all his Consols and so caused a great slump in their value. In a great panic, everybody else sold Consols. At the critical moment, he got his agents to buy all the depreciated Consols they could find, and when the news of the victory broke in London, the price of Consols soared, and he netted another fortune. Folkestone was to play a similar role again in the money market in 1844.

EFFECTS OF SMUGGLING

We have been considering the fortunes of the seafaring population so far. What was the effect of all this contraband activity on the rest of the people? As it will be imagined, the fishing industry played second fiddle. One of the crew of the 'Four Brothers' reported: 'I was born in 1800, and went to sea when about 13 years old, in fishing boats. When about 20, I joined a crew of smugglers, which brought much better pay. We had a guinea a week standing money, and for every successful voyage we had ten guineas.' This was easy money, and smuggling was much more interesting than fishing. It did not seem to occur to the men that what they were doing was reprehensible—it was just a profitable job, and this amoral sense seems to have permeated the whole community. The womenfolk supported the men implicitly, often hiding the booty and deceiving the preventive men. The whole community seemed to be involved in an unspoken conspiracy, and there was a strong resentment of interference from outside. 'Foreigners' were not welcome in the town, least of all in the eastern quarter where the smugglers had their hide-outs and escape-routes. This isolation from the rest of the country caused the people to be backward in manners and ideas, and to resist any well-meant attempts to improve things. Some of the better educated citizens were behind the efforts to improve paving and sanitation, and to make a final effort to provide a permanent harbour. In 1828 Lord Radnor made a new road along the foot of the cliffs to Sandgate. Here was an opportunity to develop a Marina and lay the foundations of a seaside resort and so bring visitors and prosperity; but the idea was not taken up until many years later. While Margate, Ramsgate and Dover leaped ahead in the new fashion for sea-bathing, Folkestone lagged behind.

A STRANGER'S IMPRESSION

We have a remarkable document which gives a picture of our forefathers at this time. It is a small note-book containing extracts copied from the notes of a retired stockbroker, named James Jenkins. He was a Quaker who came to live in Folkestone about 1820, and this is his impression of the town:

> 'Of all the places in the world known by me, none have I heard spoken so much against as Folkestone,—its ugliness has almost become proverbial,—and that I should retire from business to live in such a town has excited the wonder of some and the banter of nearly all my acquaintances. In order to prevent a continuance of these things I constantly answer the enquiries with respect to the spot I have chosen by saying that I live at Grace Hill, near Folkestone.'

Of the native inhabitants he says: 'The people in general have a wholesome and cleanly appearance, and each rank of society dress better than in most other places; women below the middling class in life often seem to display (themselves) on the first day of the week, dressed in their silks and other finery, which, I apprehend, they buy cheap.' On the whole he is tolerant of the smuggling, and notes that they do not care a rap for public opinion. Lord Liverpool 'may wish Folkestone blotted from the map of Kent because it is muck from the sea, or gone to the devil because it is a nest of detestable smugglers, but not a rush is Lord Liverpool cared for'. He notes that this indifference extended even to local authority, saying that 'magistrates bear the sword in vain, because they are open to informers'. The town abounded in young hooligans, some of whom, for example, 'pelted Alfred Jenkins, and gave Ma Cobb a blow with a stick on the back of the head, and then when she turned round, blew in her face'. He is particularly angry about unruly boys:

> 'To set about the tuition of creatures half human is beginning at the wrong end. That they often escape punishment for public crimes,—is it to be wondered at?—whilst imprudent

parents have it in their power to screen their delinquent children from justice by saying to the magistrate—"punish my child if you dare"—you know what I know and can enforce against you.'

Folkestone morals seem to have suffered a decline from the impact of smuggling, as will be seen in another connection. Jenkins observes that the men were unwilling to marry until a child was on the way. According to him, Parson Langhorne, Vicar from 1753–1772, offered a reward of a teapot to such females as came to him to be married in the virgin state. In all his time, it was claimed only once. On another occasion the Curate who was in the public reading room, announced that he had just married a couple. 'Indeed,' said one, 'in the usual circumstances?' 'Yes,' came the reply, 'there was ample and prominent proof of that.' As a corollary to this Jenkins observes that 'infanticide was not inquired into and no inquest held'. But in contrast to this we should note that there was a strong non-conformist movement growing in the town, and we shall trace this a little later on. In any case, Folkestone was probably no worse than many other places.

THE TOWN

We will now take a closer look at the town. In 1796 a private Act had been passed in Parliament for 'Paving, Repairing and Cleansing the highways, streets and lanes in the town of Folkestone'. By this a self-perpetuating Commission of Pavements had been set up to carry out various duties listed in the Act. The names of the streets were to be put up and the houses numbered; swine were not to be allowed to stray in the streets; weighing machines were to be erected to prevent the passage through the town of very heavy wagons; the markets were to be regulated and rules for keeping the streets clean were to be drawn up. The Commissioners had the right to impose fines for damage or for altering the form of the streets, and in addition to the usual highway rate, received one shilling on every chauldron of coals entering the port. But the Commissioners must have lacked authority to carry it out, for we find that in the Council Minute Book of 1836, forty years later, there is an entry:

'A practice prevails, more or less in different parts of the town, of emptying vessels in defiance of all decency from the doors and windows at all hours . . . Mr. Page should be requested to remove the line of pigsties along the church wall to another part of the premises less exposed to the public. Mr. Greig's dunghill on the Bail should be more frequently removed than appears now to be the case. Mr. Willsden, baker, should be *strongly* recommended to keep his yard in a cleaner state.'

We must remember that the town had no system of sanitation and the people still lived in a state of medieval squalor. Epidemics were frequent and infant mortality very high. In 1820 31 per cent of all deaths in the town were children under five, and they still formed 27 per cent in 1840. From time to time the town had been visited by plague; in 1720 a small-pox epidemic claimed 145 victims, and again in 1765, 158 victims; and typhoid was a frequent visitant. This is not surprising when we realize that the streets were open sewers and the sewage ran down the steep streets to accumulate at the bottom and eventually seep into the harbour. In addition many townsfolk kept pigs in their backyards and dumped their dunghills on the street.

THE POOR

The population in 1800 was still under 4,000, of whom many were very poor. Throughout the eighteenth century the overseers paid out small weekly sums ranging from 1/6 to 4/- to fifty or sixty people, mostly for the upkeep of children. For example: 'Paid Jn. Boxer jr. for keeping old Jn. Boxer's girl, 1/6 a week for 26 weeks.' Sometimes special payments were made, e.g. 'Bought three second-hand home-made shirts and gave them to Jn. Brown' or 'Paid for a creadle and churching Hatton's wife'. Many names appear repeatedly: Jn. Arnold's name appeared regularly between 1754 and 1765. Most of the money went for burials, clothing or coal.

By the end of the eighteenth century the amount of money handled by the overseers had increased enormously. In 1740 they paid out £306 9s. 6½d.; in 1786 they paid out £1,049 16s. 1½d., and despite a fall in the following year, it continued to rise until in 1824 they were paying out well over £2,000. In that year relief to the poor outside the workhouse amounted to £481 15s. 0d., with an additional £171 6s. 2d. to casual poor, non-residents and non-parishioners. Most of the remainder went on the upkeep of the Poorhouse—a new one was built in 1783—the governor's salary being £30, surgeon's bills £38, provisions £557, clothing £124 and so on. To pay for this fourteen rates were raised bringing in £1,791. We must remember that as we said, the population was still under 4,000, but, in fact, the rate books show that this sum of money was being raised from approximately 800 people. In 1823 they were paying about £183 every month, some people paying as much as £1 a month, and one man paying over £8 a month. This was quite apart from the rate raised by the Commissioners for Pavements and the town rate.

It was these more responsible and conscientious citizens who strove to better conditions in the town. Not all were corrupted by the blight of smuggling and permissiveness. There were a number of honest, clean-living people like William Fagg, a sailor who was pressed into the navy in 1803, and rose to be master of the cutter 'Flora'. He operated a service between London and Calais for several years, and later on between London and Rotterdam; and his letters home to his wife living in Folkestone at Rosemary Lane reveal a simple and homely affection, and a pride in their small son. Jenkins comments on the homeliness of some of the Folkestone men, and how they even hung out the family washing. Another peculiarity he mentions was the fact that although Folkestone was a fishing town, it was difficult to buy fresh fish. All the catch was dried or smoked and so there was a constant odour of stale fish, but no fresh fish.

NON-CONFORMIST MOVEMENT

There was, as we have said, during the eighteenth century a growing non-conformist movement; the services in the parish church were ill attended, and consisted of a duet between the parson and the clerk, and many people especially the non-conformists resented the payment of church rates. The growth of the Baptist Church in Folkestone illustrates how a new religious movement came to interest some of the more serious-minded citizens. About 1720 a number of Baptists used to meet every Sunday in the parlour of Mr. John Stace at Bradstone Mill. Apparently about 1724 there were six other Folkestone residents who used regularly to travel to a Baptist

Meeting House in Canterbury every Sunday; and in 1728 a number of Baptists from Hythe joined Mr. Stace with the intention of forming a Particular Baptist Church in Folkestone. In 1729 he gave a piece of ground in Mill Bay, upon which they subsequently built a meeting house. This building continued in use until 1845, when the Baptists bought a new site in Rendezvous Street where they erected Salem Chapel, replaced in 1873 by the present building. Another group of Baptists, called Strict Baptists, used to meet as early as 1698 in Thomas Carr's house; and in 1701 they moved to J. Kennett's house by the Bayle Pond.

Another non-conformist group who developed early on were the Society of Friends, or Quakers. A burial ground was granted to them as early as 1671, on the site of the present Meeting House. There is a reference in the town records to their Meeting House in 1684, when the Mayor and Jurats had their doors locked, thus testifying to local opposition. But the Quakers were particularly severe on their members who were guilty of immorality. They built themselves a new Meeting House in 1790 at a cost of £616 6s. 8d., a fact which suggests that they were fairly wealthy. This building, refronted, still stands in the old Dover Street, now known as Harbour Way.

The Congregationalists were an off-shoot from the Folkestone Anabaptists, and in 1797 they established themselves as an independent community under the patronage of the Countess of Huntingdon, meeting at first in the Zion Chapel in Fancy Street. Their church in Tontine Street was built in 1856, and subsequently enlarged. Meanwhile a group of Wesleyan Methodists was formed in 1824, meeting in a large room in Elgar's Yard, close to the harbour. They erected a chapel in High Street in 1831 (still in use as a club), and subsequently built another chapel in Sandgate Road, next to the King's Arms (1852). When in 1864 Folkestone was designated the head of a 'circuit' the Wesleyans built a large and handsome church with a lofty spire at the junction of Grace Hill and Dover Road (formerly Mill Lane). This church was built at the national expense to cater for the growing congregations of visitors to the town during the holiday season. The Primitive Methodists, the Plymouth Brethren and the Roman Catholics also had their own churches.

We have mentioned these religious groups to indicate a growing resistance to the permissiveness and immorality which was rife throughout the eighteenth century and at the beginning of the nineteenth century. The impact of smuggling, cheap liquor and easy money certainly demoralized the community, so that family life tended to break up, men were loth to take on the responsibilities of marriage unless forced into it, and the number of illegitimate births far exceeded the number of legitimate ones. From 1750 onwards the number gave rise to consternation, not so much on moral grounds but because of the effect on the poor rate. Between 1780 and 1800 there were 104 bastards born. No wonder Parson Langhorne's teapot went unclaimed! We have seen how the poor rate soared at the beginning of the nineteenth century, and how the town abounded in unruly and uncouth urchins. Several of the non-conformist churches ran Sunday schools, the Baptists opening theirs in Mill Bay as early as 1818; and others followed suit. In the course of the century other factors combined to lift the population from its insularity and ignorance, notably the coming of the railway, the change in duty rates, the influx of a new population and the impact of compulsory schooling.

It is not to be supposed that in this period the majority of Folkestone people were uncouth and demoralized. There was a body of responsible citizens who carried on the burden of local government against considerable odds, and it was these who did their utmost to improve conditions in the town.

AMUSEMENTS

But it must be admitted that there was little in the way of entertainment available for the ordinary people. There were plenty of taverns—about forty of them—where convivial company might be found. And on special occasions, which were fully advertised in the County papers, there were cock-fighting bouts of long duration. For example, in 1766 'At the Fountain on the 19th May will be fought a welch main of cocks for a silver quart pot, value £8 - 12 - 0; sixteen cocks to be entered, 7/6 entrance fee for each. Cocks to be paired by ticket, and fight till but one winner.' Again, 'On Saturday, 15th March 1769, at the White Hart in Folkestone, (Mr. Charles Hills), between the Gentlemen of Canterbury and of Folkestone.' These fights were staged at many of the taverns until as late as 1849, when they were banned because of their cruelty. The fighting cocks were armed with steel spurs one to two inches long.

During the early summer Folkestone families used to repair to the Cherry Gardens for picnics and for the cherry crop. This was done for the greater part of the eighteenth century and for the first half of the nineteenth. *Tiffin's Guide* (1816) tells us of 'a cottage half hidden among the trees' used as a house of refreshment with dancing in the evening. In the cherry season visitors were allowed to pick and eat as many cherries as they liked, but they could take none away in baskets. The cottage was replaced by a tavern and latterly by a tea-house. It was closed in 1869.

The town seems to have celebrated Royal occasions with some gusto as we learn from the *Kentish Gazette* for 2nd June, 1770:

> 'We hear from Folkestone that on Monday, the 4th inst being his Majesty's birthday, will be played off there a very curious set of fireworks, consisting of fountains, sky rockets, catherine wheels of various forms; several curious pieces of machinery, and also a representation of a swan, which is to swim on the water and playing fireworks from its body at the same time.'

On the accession of Queen Victoria the arrangements for the Proclamation ceremony were laid out in great detail. The Minutes of the Meeting of the Town Council for 23rd June, 1837 read thus:

> 'Resolved that the Proclamation of her Majesty Queen Victoria do take place tomorrow at two o'clock in the afternoon and that the Order of Procession for that purpose be as follows, viz
>
> Constables two and two
> Colors flying
> Band of Music
> Town Sergeant
> Two Constables to clear the Way
> Town Clerk on Horseback with the Proclamation
> The Mayor, Minister & Aldermen two and two
> Councillors two and two.
>
> Resolved that the procession do move from the Guildhall to the Centre of Sandgate Road (where Proclamation be read)— thence return to the Market Place (where Proclamation be read)—thence to the Bail at the corner nearest the Church Yard

(where Proclamation be read) thence along the Bail down Bail Street to the Folkestone Arms (where Proclamation be read)—thence down High Street through Queen's Place to about the commencement of Radnor Street (where Proclamation be read)—thence up Seagate Street to about the centre of Dover Street (where Proclamation be read)—thence up Dover Street, down to Mill Lane up Rendezvous Street to the Rose (where Proclamation be read).

Ordered that the Treasurer pay the Band Two Pounds—the Ringers One Pound and ten shillings and to each of the Constables employed Two shillings and six pence.

Ordered that the underwritten Notice of the Proclamation be given generally to the Cryer of Folkestone this afternoon and tomorrow morning and that he be paid two shillings and sixpence for his trouble. And that the like notice by the Cryer of Sandgate be given there and that he be paid two shillings for his trouble.'

It is interesting to follow the route of the procession as it indicates the limits of the town at the time.

MARTELLO TOWERS

One feature of the Folkestone scene which appeared at the beginning of the nineteenth century was the line of Martello Towers, erected 1805–6. These were yet another scheme of defence against invasion, this time against Napoleon. The towers stretched from East Wear Bay to Seaford in Sussex. They were built of brick with walls 8 feet thick on an average. The roofs were supported on a central column 5 feet in diameter, on which was mounted a traversing gun which moved round a central pivot. The name Martello was a corruption of the word Mortella, the name of a tower in Corsica, on which these towers were modelled. Many of them still stand at intervals along the coast and deserve to be protected as monuments of our past history.

PART III

MODERN FOLKESTONE

CHAPTER SEVEN

THE BUILDING OF THE HARBOUR

THROUGHOUT the eighteenth century the condition of the Stade deteriorated, and attempt after attempt was made to protect it. In November, 1703, a terrible storm carried away one boat and damaged many others, sweeping away the beach, tearing up the capstans, and undermining the foundations of several houses. In 1709 conditions were so bad that fears were felt for the very existence of the fishery. A Mr. Markwick, the engineer of Romney Marsh was called in, and he advised the erection of three jetties of timber and stone, which would cause a lodgement of the 'swarve' for the Stade, and a protection of the cliff below the parish church. The fishermen offered to pay for the cost, an estimated £600, by a voluntary contribution of 6d. in the pound of the value of their catch. And the Corporation sought leave of the new lord of the manor, Jacob des Bouverie, Esq. to place the jetties along the shore and to use stone taken from his quarries.

Another storm in December, 1724, finally demolished these jetties, causing damage to the extent of £1,100—a sum which the poor fishermen could not raise for their repair. Mackie reports:

> 'So reduced were the inhabitants by these incessant and heavy losses, that in April, 1725, they petitioned the Lords Commissioners of the Great Seal to take their deplorable circumstances into consideration, and to grant them letters patent to enable them to collect charitable contributions throughout the kingdom for the relief and support of the poor sufferers and their families, that they might not come to utter ruin and dispersion. This petition affords us much information on the state of the town. It tells us that there were then engaged in the fishery about 240 persons, most of them very poor and barely subsisting by their employment: that the stade, or station for their boats, was an open strand, upon which they were drawn up by capstans, that had previously been well secured by two points of land jutting out into the sea, by the wasting away of which it at length became exposed to the action of the waves.'

We do not know what help, if any, was provided as the result of this appeal.

In 1766 it was found necessary to act again in repairing the jetties. An Act of Parliament was obtained 'for the support and preservation of the Parish Church of Folkestone, and the lower part of the town from the ravages of the sea'. It was feared that the West Cliff would be undermined, thus endangering the church; and it was hoped that a new jetty would cause the beach to collect at the base of the cliff. To meet the cost of building and maintenance a duty was levied on all coal brought into the town. The new jetty was built by Richard Elgar, who supplied the wood for it, and the work began on the site of the present Paris Hotel. In 1771 it had to be repaired, and five years later it was too ruinous to be worth repairing. Between 1787 and 1799 four more jetties were built, and demolished by the sea, and so ended another century of disaster.

THE HAVEN

It was realized at last that the only solution was to erect a stone-built haven in which ships could be moored or ride at anchor without danger from the waves. In 1804 a petition was presented to Parliament by Lord Radnor, asking leave to build the proposed harbour. In 1807 an Act was obtained 'for constructing a Pier and Harbour at or near the town of Folkestone'. A Folkestone Harbour Company was floated with a capital of £22,000, and most of the responsible and wealthier citizens of the town bought £50 shares.

There is some doubt as to who was the original designer of the Folkestone Harbour; most of the contemporary guide books give the credit to Thomas Telford, the famous engineer, but he seems to have been consulted at a much later date, in 1817 and again in 1829. The existing plans in the Folkestone Museum are signed by William Jessup, possibly a partner in the firm of Rennie and Jessup, which built Margate Harbour. Mackie refers to some plans and estimates prepared by Mr. Henry Cull, which were presented to Lord Radnor. Nevertheless it is important to realize that several schemes had been prepared and debated from 1803 onwards, and the plans were modified on the grounds of expense. The original plan for the

haven projected a long breakwater pier from Copt Point westwards along the ridge of the Whelk Shell Rocks; and a second
pier running out from a point west of the Pent stream, and
turning at right-angles eastwards to approach the other pier.
(Fig. 2.) This would provide a large haven of about 30 acres, but

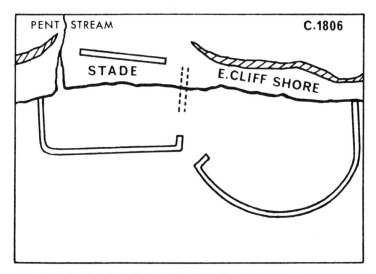

FIG. 2. William Jessup's original plan enclosing an area of 30 acres.

the scheme was too ambitious. So Jessup produced another plan
which reduced the area by projecting an eastern pier from
the East Sands, and a small breakwater between the heads of
the piers, based on the Stake Ness Rocks which were a known
hazard to shipping. (Fig. 3.) Finally, this plan was reduced to
the western pier with its right-angled return pier only. A short
breakwater, at first unconnected to the shore, was added later.
(Fig. 4.)

THE BUILDING OF THE PIER

It was decided that the stones forming the pier should be
laid one above the other at an angle of 45 degrees, and left
without cement, so that they would offer less resistance to the
waves. So the work was begun, very slowly at first, as it was
carried out with manual labour aided only by a derrick. As

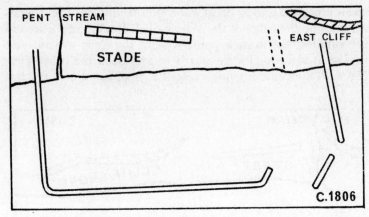

FIG. 3. Jessup's second plan, with a breakwater based on the Stake Ness Rocks.

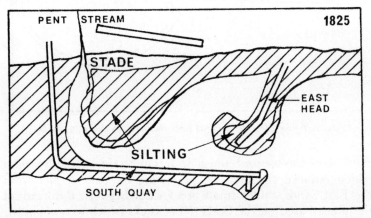

FIG. 4. The harbour as eventually built, c. 1820. The shading indicates the areas which became choked with silt.

the pier grew it checked the flow of sand and shingle from the west, and a growing extent of land was formed which protected the cliffs and the Stade. Eventually, when the first pier was finished a spit of shingle was deposited by the tide along from the pier head and parallel with the seashore. This spit served as a foundation for the south pier which was built next. Finally, a breakwater was built on the eastern side of the haven to protect ships from easterly gales.

So, at last, the town had a haven for its ships, and it was hoped that there would be an increase of trade through the harbour. For a time there was an increase, and what the piers meant to trading vessels may be seen from the following extract:

> 'On Wednesday last (January 19th. 1810) was shipped by Mr. A. H. Spratt, of Canterbury, on board the Perseverence, sloop, of 60 tons . . . from the western pierhead of Folkestone Harbour, a cargo of paving stones for London. This being the first shipment, the workmen belonging to the harbour, to the quarry and to the ship, drank "prosperity to the undertaking", and gave three times three cheers from the pierhead. The advantages of this work are placed beyond doubt by this experiment, and the shipment was effected in six hours in perfect safety, and which would have taken some days of exposure in an open and dangerous coast.'

Thus as early as 1810 the solid advantages of a stone pier were demonstrated; and by 1820 the little haven enclosing 14 acres was complete. There was a small increase in trade and the population of the town grew slightly. But there was an unexpected set-back in the following years. The sea deposited at each high tide a layer of sand and shingle, which, over the next ten years almost completely choked the harbour, and there was only a small channel alongside the south quay where the Pent stream trickled out. In fact the harbour was navigable to a very limited extent only at high tide, on account of the huge bar of sand that had accumulated at the mouth of the port. A great deal of money was expended on digging out the shingle by manual labour, and several schemes were proposed for remedying the difficulty. One scheme, suggested by Thomas Telford, was to construct another pier parallel with the south quay from the end of the East Head, and to build a sluice to retain a pool of sea-water at low tide, thus forming a large wet-dock for trading vessels. (Fig. 5.) This, and other schemes, were considered, but they were far too costly for the Harbour Company to undertake. After expending the whole of their capital of £59,500, they obtained a further £10,000 on a mortgage from the Government; but in 1842 the Company went bankrupt, and all the great hopes of trade and prosperity had vanished. The Government put the harbour up for sale.

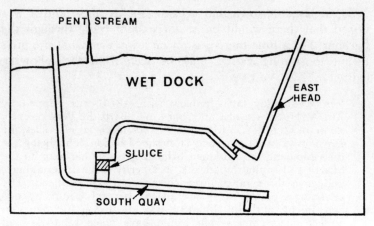

Fig. 5. To render the harbour fully practicable again, Thomas Telford proposed a system of sluices to create a wet dock (1829).

THE RAILWAY ARRIVES

It was at this point that the tide of fortune turned. In 1836 the South Eastern Railway Company had been granted permission by Act of Parliament to build a railway from London to Dover. By 1842 the railway engineers were approaching the hinterland of Folkestone, and were already constructing the difficult stretch of line between Folkestone and Dover. There were disputes with the Dover Harbour Board about the siting of the Dover Station and the use of the Dover pier. When Folkestone Harbour was offered for sale, the Directors of the Railway Company immediately saw the advantages they would have if they possessed a harbour of their own. They would not have to pay harbour dues to another concern and they could arrange their train services to suit the boat sailings. The Railway Company bought the harbour for the bargain price of £18,000, and proceeded to clear out the shingle and restore the whole basin to its full use. There was one difficulty still outstanding. The Company had not planned to include Folkestone Harbour on its route, and the line was being constructed at least a mile inland from the town as it then was. In 1842 the railway engineers were building the great viaduct over the Foord Valley, and the Chief Engineer, William Cubitt, had to incorporate the harbour into his plans. So a railway junction and station was built at the east end of the viaduct, and a subsidiary line (called the 'tram road') was built in 1843, to connect with the Harbour. At first this line was regarded merely as a means of conveying coal from the harbour to the coking sheds near the East Station—hence the name 'tram road' which implies a road or line for carrying minerals only. Coal was brought by colliers from Tyneside and unloaded at the little jetty in the harbour, specially built by the railway engineers for transporting coal up to the coke ovens. At this time all locomotives had to be driven by smokeless fuel to satisfy local objections to smoke and sparks, and the Company proposed to use Folkestone as its chief source of coke for all its locomotives. So colliers were dispatched from Tyneside and they unloaded their coal at the Harbour, thus bringing work and profit to the town.

THE CROSS-CHANNEL SERVICE

The South Eastern Railway Company next sought to initiate a cross-channel steamship service from Folkestone to Boulogne. They had, first, to employ steamers belonging to the 'New Commercial Steam Packet Company' as they had not obtained the necessary powers from Parliament to run a steamer service of their own. So they chartered the 'City of Boulogne', the 'Sir William Wallace', and the 'Emerald' to start the service, which was inaugurated on 1st August, 1843, the public opening of the railway line to Folkestone having taken place on 24th June, 1843. A further factor in the plan for the cross-channel service was the fact that the Railway Company invested capital in the building of the railway line from Boulogne to Amiens, thus ensuring a continuous rail journey to Paris. No such railway existed between Calais and Paris on the Dover route, and so Folkestone suddenly became within the space of a few months the most important link with the continent. It was now possible to travel from London to Paris via Folkestone in a matter of 12 hours: any other route took days.

When the railway was opened there were six trains daily to London, each way, and the fastest took 2 hours 50 minutes to do the 87¾ miles via Croydon, Reigate and Tonbridge. As for the fare, the first class rail fare to London was 15/-; by contrast, the stage coach fare was 30/- inside and 16/- outside, the journey by coach taking twelve hours. There is no wonder that Folkestone suddenly became a place of importance, and travellers began to flock through the port. They noticed that it had scenic attractions—high cliffs, a sandy foreshore, some bathing machines, and a delightful setting of hills and valleys behind. To accommodate any of the travellers who were inclined to stay a night or two, the Railway Company built in 1843 the most efficient and up-to-date hotel on the south coast—the Pavilion Hotel, which became in itself an attraction to discerning visitors.

WILLIAM CUBITT

The presiding genius behind all these developments was William Cubitt, who did more to modernise Folkestone and bring it prosperity than any other person of the time. He not only pioneered the perfectly straight railway line from Reigate to Ashford, but negotiated the Folkestone region with his impressive viaduct, and the difficult Warren stretch with its four tunnels; he even removed a whole hill called 'Round Down Cliff', by means of explosives. The building of the branch line to the Harbour, and the subsequent installation of the swing bridge and the Harbour Station was done according to his plans; and his design for making a deep-water harbour beyond the already existing haven, although never put into effect, was far more ambitious and promising than any subsequent development. (Fig. 6.) He was a truly great engineer whose achievements have never been fully recognized.

But we anticipate. Between 1843 and 1849 travellers wishing to catch the boat had to alight at the Junction Station, and walk to the harbour—or take the ramshackle horse-bus down the steep streets. Charles Dickens who visited Folkestone in the early days has some amusing comments upon the hardships of the first travellers in his article 'Out of Town', which he wrote for his *Household Words*. To avoid these discomforts the Company sought powers to convey passengers down the branch-line of the Tramroad; and the first swing-bridge was therefore installed in 1849 and a new station built out over the beach of the foreshore beyond the South Quay. (Fig. 7.) Passengers could now stay in the train and alight on the very quay itself—a great convenience. And so almost by accident Folkestone got a

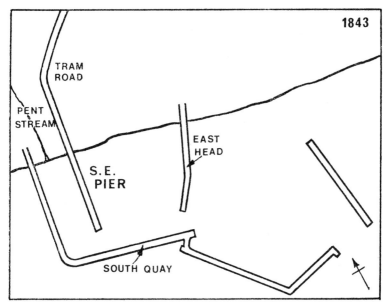

FIG. 6. In 1843 William Cubitt made a plan to extend the whole harbour for future development. Only the 'Tram Road' and the S.E. Jetty were actually constructed.

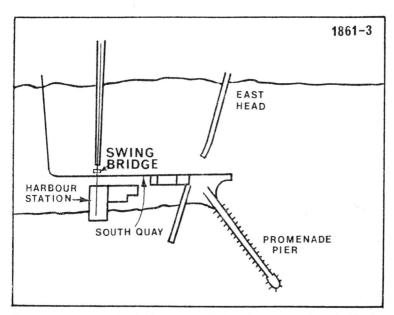

FIG. 7. In 1849 the swing bridge was installed, and between 1861 and 1863 the Promenade Pier was built.

station, actually in or close to the town, and for many years this was the most popular point of departure for the towns-folk too.

THE INDIA MAIL

A further factor which helped to increase the traffic through Folkestone Harbour was the diversion of the India Mail from Dover to Folkestone. The India Mail consisted of advance information abóut current prices of various commodities in the Indian markets which were already on their way to London. Speed was essential, and a knowledge of the various prices was important to London commercial houses and to the Stock Exchange. By sending the Mail via Folkestone at least twelve hours could be saved, as in 1844 the railway line from Folkestone to London was open, but not as yet from Dover.

The India Mail was made up at Bombay and carried by ship and carts to Marseilles, where an abstract of the India news was drawn up for the information of the French and English governments. This abstract was sent by telegraph to Paris and thence to Boulogne, where it was put on the steamer for Folkestone. The passage by the Dover steam boats had varied from 2 hours and 40 minutes to 14 hours; and by sailing vessels from 3 hours 55 minutes to 48 hours. The S.E. Railway hoped to be able to send the Mail by their new steamers to Folkestone in at most 1 hour 45 minutes. Something of the excitement of the time can be gleaned from this report from the *Illustrated London News* for 6th July, 1844:

'Immediately on the Mail signal being observed, the railway harbour-master, the indefatigable Mr. Faulkner, makes the necessary arrangements for its reception. If it be high water these are simple and commonplace enough, as the dispatch has merely to be landed and sent by the Mail omnibus to the (Junction) Station, a journey of about a mile, performed amid the shouts of the company, who usually assemble in great numbers to welcome its arrival—at the breakneck pace of twenty miles an hour. But if it be low water, the weather rough, and the time night, a scene of exciting adventure ensues. A galley—a long clear-water boat, manned by some eight or more stout fellows, under Mr. Faulkner's command—is launched from the beach, and sent off to the approaching vessel. On reaching it, a large blue light is fired, and in the glare of its ghostly fume, the captain of the steamer descends, bearing the express, and is immediately rowed to the shore, when, if it be dark, and a heavy surf rolling, a number of fishermen are usually posted with flambeaus to light them through the breakers. On landing, the express is committed to Mr. Faulkner, who carries it to the train.'

These were brave days and the reporter obviously made the most of the occasion. And the whole of Folkestone used to turn out in their Sunday best, top-hats and all, to cheer the mail on its arrival (see frontispiece). The Railway Company set out to make the most of the port with its new Pavilion Hotel, its handsome Harbour Offices with the Clock tower in Venetian style, and its convenient arrangements for conveying passengers' luggage through the Customs. The last were in operation from 1849 onwards when passengers were conveyed down the Harbour Branch line direct to the quayside by train.

NEW CUSTOM HOUSE

After 1849 the passenger traffic increased so much that in 1854 the Company erected a new Custom House on the south quay for the convenience of travellers. This development was enthusiastically reported in the *Illustrated London News*, as follows:

'The new works erected by the South-Eastern Railway Company at Folkestone Harbour for the accommodation of passengers may be considered to be among the best arranged in England, if not in Europe.

The first block of buildings commences at the railway station, and extends in an easterly direction two hundred and three feet towards the lighthouse, terminating with a very handsome and commodious Custom House—the whole facing towards the harbour, and in perfect harmony of style in its architectural design. That portion of the building immediately adjoining the station is devoted to the examination of baggage, and measures 118 feet in length by 46 in breadth, having a handsome portal, with lofty and massive oak doors in the centre, through which the baggage is admitted.

At the eastern end of the building, and immediately adjoining the Custom House, is another noble entrance, leading through a lofty hall into the general waiting-room. On the right of the waiting room is the refreshment room, equally commodious; and facing the sea is a long corridor leading direct to the ladies' waiting-room, ticket office, and station platform. The whole of the doors, as well as the furniture, are of solid oak, and harmonise well with the simple yet handsome interior of the building.'

Charles Dickens testified to the efficiency of the services in
his essay 'Out of Town'. Here he describes Folkestone as he knew
it in the early fifties, and he comments on the great activity at
the harbour:

> 'Now, after infinite bustle, the steamer steams out, and we (on
> the pier) are all delighted when she rolls as if she would roll her
> funnel out, and are all disappointed when she don't. Now the
> other steamer is coming in, and the custom house prepares,
> and the wharf-labourers assemble, and the hawsers are made
> ready, and the hotel porters come rattling down with van and
> truck, eager to begin more Olympic games with more luggage.'

It is no wonder that the Folkestone service grew by leaps and
bounds, and that travellers preferred to cross the Channel by
the Folkestone boats. A glance at the following records shows
how the Folkestone and Dover passenger traffic increased in
these years:

Dover–Calais		Folkestone–Boulogne
1845	18,642	70,809
1850	54,036	82,016
1855	80,413	134,633 (Paris Exhibition)
1860	76,318	96,652
1865	133,532	118,553

Similarly the Customs revenue increased rapidly as these
figures show: 1847—£4,800; 1848—£8,000; 1849—£42,260;
1850—£79,000; 1854—£140,000. Again, as we should expect,
there was a growth of population over these years:

1801	3,257	1841	3,723
1811	3,697	1851	6,726
1821	3,989	1861	8,507
1831	3,638	1871	11,304

There was an unexpected decline between 1821 and 1841,
possibly due to the silting up of the harbour and the consequent
loss of trade; it was swiftly repaired when the railway took
charge, but there was a fear that the decline might be repeated
as another huge bar of sand grew at the harbour mouth. This
fear is expressed in the following extract:

> 'And whether a serviceable harbour can be maintained here
> remains to be seen. It is a tidal harbour of 14 acres area and
> perhaps is sufficiently under engineering control; but it already

PLATE 17. The bottom of Sandgate Road (formerly Cow Street), showing the old Sessions House. (Folkestone Museum.)

PLATE 18. The same scene, *c.* 1865. (Folkestone Museum.)

PLATE 19. The site of Bouverie Square, showing Bouverie Lodge under construction and the windmill in Millfield. (Detail from a painting by R. J. Lonsdale, Folkestone Museum.)

PLATE 20. Bouverie Square, 1862. Bouverie Lodge on the right. (Old engraving.)

PLATE 21. The Lower Sandgate Road and the West Cliff Estate. (From a lithograph, c. 1860.) Note the Leas, still unbuilt apart from Nos. 1 and 2. On the right are the Parish Church, Albion Villas, West Cliff Gardens and the upper part of Sandgate Road as far as Christ Church on the left.

PLATE 22. Christ Church as first built in 1850. Windmill on the left. (Folkestone Museum.)

PLATE 23. Early Bathing Machines on foreshore and Lower Sandgate Road, *c.* 1860. (Watercolour, Folkestone Museum.)

PLATE 24. Early Bathing Machine and Willis's Warm Baths at the foot of the Slope Road, August, 1846. (Watercolour, Folkestone Museum.)

shows something like a determination to silt up. Then the continual tendency of the shingle to form a bar at the mouth of the harbour has to be overcome; and, to do so even temporarily, it has been found necessary to employ 200 men at a time. A groin has been run out from the westward for the purpose of arresting the progress of the shingle, but it is not likely to do so for many years. Still, as the difficulties are so well known, it is probable that sufficient means may be found of providing against them; and we hope modern science will be found more efficient than the old corporation muster.' (*The Land We Live In*: Vol. II, p. 135, *c.* 1860.)

THE PROBLEM OF THE BAR

Sufficient means have never been found to avoid the silting up of the harbour; but a means of circumventing the difficulty was found by adopting the first part of William Cubitt's plan. The first steamers were quite small and could sail only when the tide was full enough to enable them to surmount the bar. Both Folkestone and Boulogne harbours were troubled with this problem, and it was a popular pastime to see the boat breast the waves as she went over the bar. We have seen a reference to it in Dickens's comment above; here is another description taken from the *Illustrated Times* for 4th September, 1858:

'The Folkestone Boat will soon be off; and as there is "a rough sea on", let us go and see how she will meet the tremendous swell which is dashing over the pier head. The balls on the mast-head at the Lighthouse show that the water is sufficiently high, and therefore in a few minutes she will start. It has been blowing hard all night from the north, and the wind has churned up the sea into a state of turbulence and commotion, which make a voyage across the Channel, in the teeth of wind and tide, by no means a pleasant prospect to bad sailors. But as I was not going, I could afford to enjoy the sight. The water in Boulogne harbour is, I should fancy, mostly smooth; but just outside there is a bar of sand, and when the tide is coming in, with a strong wind behind it, the waves rise over the bar to a great height. And when these light Folkestone steamers— made, as they are, especially for speed—dash at these waves, it is a sight worth seeing. On this occasion the sea was un- commonly rough; the waves along the line at the mouth of the port literally appeared to run mountains high. Swiftly and smoothly, with full steam on, came the boat, and when she attacked the waves, it seemed as if she must be buried in the water; but she rose like a cork, lifting her prow out of the waves as if she would come right over, just as I have seen a rearing horse overbalance himself and fall backwards. But, no! her prow now pitches downwards, and up goes her stern, and the first great line of waves is surmounted; but from what I could see, not until the decks had been swept fore and aft, the passengers thoroughly drenched, and "the stomach pump" of bad sailors like myself, set in motion. For miles away I could see her riding joyously on the waves; sometimes lifting her stern so high that I could see her keel, and anon so buried in the trough of the sea, that nothing but her funnel and masts were visible. It was a fine sight, that little boat dashing over he waters against wind and tide. Forty years ago no ship could have left the harbour, but now, in despite of wind and tide, in two hours and a quarter this dashing little boat will be across the channel.'

A NEW PIER

It was soon clear that the Company needed to use larger boats which could sail at any state of the tide. Following Cubitt's idea a new jetty was thrown out from the end of the south quay into deeper water to take the larger steamers. Hence the building of the 'Promenade Pier' (1861–1863), so called because visitors could walk out to sea and watch the steamers come in. It was at first a modest affair made of solid timber, but it served its purpose well as a low water landing stage and the number of passengers increased by leaps and bounds. The railway company purchased two new steamers to take the increasing numbers, the 'Victoria' and the 'Albert Edward'. They were much larger, having two funnels and masts, well raked, and clipper bows, and were very handsome vessels. A few years later a third boat of similar design was added to the service, the 'Napoleon III'. After 1863 the pier extension was strengthened with iron girders and completed with a lighthouse. But there was one inconvenience to travellers. On rough, windy days they were exposed to the weather, and they were liable to get a wetting from the waves splashing over the open deck of the pier. Besides, it was a considerable walk to the shelter of the Custom House and the terminal railway station. Obviously something more substantial was needed to protect passengers, and the engineers and directors of the railway spent the next years in planning further developments.

A further impetus to the expansion of the Folkestone Harbour came from the rivalry of the new East Kent Railway which reached Dover in 1862. Just at this juncture the new railway, soon to be known as the London, Chatham and Dover Railway, obtained the Government contract for the conveyance of the mail from London to the French coast. The South Eastern directors had foolishly refused the contract, as they thought it unprofitable, and were now regretting the great chance they had ceded to their rivals. In 1866 the South Eastern Company elected Sir Edward Watkin Chairman of the Board. Watkin was a dynamic personality who was determined to get the better of the rival railway company, and the next thirty years saw a period of intense competition between them. The first concern of the South Eastern was to eclipse the facilities of Dover Harbour by building on a large scale at Folkestone.

WATKIN'S PLANS

Watkin's first aim was to avoid the inconvenient reversal of direction which the boat trains had to make at the Junction Station, and the further steep gradient from the Junction to the Harbour station—a fall of 111 feet in 1,328 yards. In 1862 he proposed to build a new line starting from a point west of Shorncliffe Station, and running in a detour north of the main Dover line, through the arches of the Foord viaduct and so down the Pent valley to the Harbour. There was strong opposition from local residents, and the scheme was abandoned. Later, he built a branch line from Sandling to Hythe (1872) and Sandgate (1874) with the intention of extending it along the Lower Sandgate Road to the Harbour. The Lord of the Manor and the town opposed this last scheme, and so the peace and beauty of Folkestone's Leas and foreshore were not shattered by the encroaching railway. And Boat trains still have to negotiate the formidable incline of the Harbour Branch, and make the reversal of direction at the junction.

Watkin's other scheme was to increase the size of the Harbour by running a long pier from the Copt rocks westward, and building another to meet it on the west side of the pier extension, thus enclosing a vast acreage of water. This was an enlargement of Jessup's original plan, and very similar to that proposed by Cubitt in 1843. But such grandiose schemes were regarded with disfavour by the Admiralty, since Folkestone would then become a superior port to Dover, which had always been

considered the more important, as the seat of the Lord Warden
of the Cinque Ports and an important naval base. So Watkin's
scheme again came to nought, and he had the further annoy-
ance of seeing his scheme, or something similar, carried out at
Dover. A further project was to provide a long breakwater pier
to the west of the open promenade pier, so protecting the latter

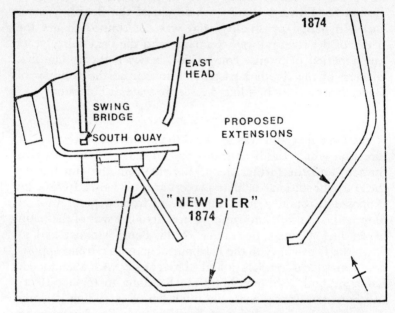

Fig. 8. Sir Edward Watkin's ambitious plans for enlarging the whole harbour.
They were abandoned and the 'New Pier' was extended instead.

from the rough seas; but even this had to be abandoned in
favour of an extension and rebuilding of the existing pier.
(Fig. 8).

THE 'NEW PIER'

To avoid the inconvenience to travellers of walking the
length of the old pier, the railway track was extended from the
end of the terminal station and run on to the pier itself. This
enabled travellers to transfer from the train to the boat in
comparative comfort. In succeeding years the pier was strengthened and improved, but there still remained the exposure to

the elements. In 1881 it was decided to enclose the old structure in a cladding of stone and to make a protecting parapet on the western side. A single-line station platform was erected under a canopy or roof projecting from the parapet, and better facilities made for handling the cross-channel traffic. The pier, now called the 'New Pier' was further extended and opened in 1883. The south quay tended to be used for cargo vessels only, except at high tides or peak periods of traffic. Colliers and coastal vessels still used the Inner and Outer Harbours of the old port, and maintained a flourishing trade for many years. During the 1860's the Railway Company built a fish quay along the Stade, erected a repair shop, and a short jetty alongside the old East Head where boat repairs could be carried out; and they built a gridiron pier at right angles to the Tramroad arches. Eventually Folkestone Harbour became a very flourishing concern, importing 14 million tons of merchandise annually, and the sight of all the sailing and steam boats crowding the harbour was an attraction to visitors for many years.

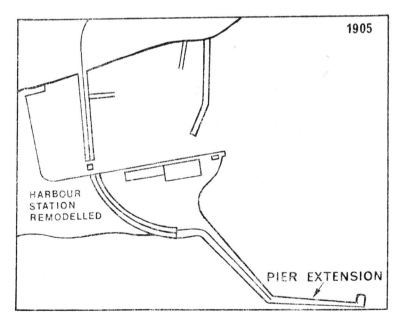

1905

HARBOUR
STATION
REMODELLED

PIER EXTENSION

FIG. 9. The final extension of the pier was made between 1897 and 1905.

THE LAST EXTENSION

The passenger traffic continued to grow, necessitating further developments. These were carried out between 1897 and 1905. The New Pier was extended in an east-south-easterly direction and the pier station was provided with two lines and a double awning. The structure of the existing pier needed much repair after its years of service, and so it was decided to rebuild it in the form of a masonry breakwater and extend the whole. A promenade was provided on the western side as far as the lighthouse, and extra emergency berths were incorporated into the western side. This pier has proved to be sufficient for all needs until very recently (1972). (Fig. 9.)

In 1899 the long rivalry between the two Kent railways came to an end and they were amalgamated under the name of 'The South Eastern and Chatham Railway'. The Railway Company's Offices with their clock tower—a well-known landmark—were demolished and the Pavilion Hotel was enlarged and rebuilt in brick and terra cotta. In 1903 the first turbine steamer, the 'Queen' came into operation, thus ushering in the twentieth century. The old paddle steamers continued for a while, some of them being employed in coastal traffic and summer excursions.

Additional Note to Page 79

Further evidence of the depredations of the sea may be gleaned from *The Gentleman's Magazine*, Vol. XIX (1749) page 43: 'great damages have been done this month (January) by the high winds and floods . . . At *Folkstone* in *Kent*, on the 11th, the wind strong at S.W. and a spring tide, attended with an extraordinary swell (the tide running with the wind), the surge of the sea carried away almost all the beach from before the town . . . On the 12th the tide wash'd away part of a house, at the south head of the town, and smash'd the boats. His majesty's watch-house was in so much danger that the officers quitted it; when the tide abated, the beach was clean carried away, almost knee-deep all along the town. Goods were washed out of the houses, as coppers, barrels, tubs, wearing cloaths, etc. and so many capsterns torn up, that the damage of them is £150 and the whole near £1,000.'

CHAPTER EIGHT

THE BIRTH OF A SEASIDE RESORT

WE have already quoted Quaker Jenkins's opinions of Folkestone in his time and the reputation it had in other places. There is abundant evidence to substantiate his views. In 1805 the Duke of Rutland published a *Journal of a Tour Round the Southern Coasts of England* and observed: 'It appears a dirty town, nor does it seem to possess any thing to induce the passing traveller to stop within it.' The idea that it should aspire to become a fashionable resort was received with incredulous amusement. Thomas Ingoldsby's comments deserve to be quoted in this connection:

> 'Not many miles removed from the verge of this recondite region, (Romney Marsh) stands a collection of houses, which its maligners call a fishing town, and its well-wishers a Watering Place. A limb of one of the Cinque Ports, it has, (or lately had), a corporation of its own, and has been thought considerable enough to give a second title to a noble family . . . At the eastern extremity of the town, on the sea-beach, and scarcely above high-water mark, stood, in the good old times, a row of houses then denominated 'Frog-hole'. Modern refinement subsequently euphonised the name into "East-street;" but "what's in a name?" the encroachments of Ocean have long since levelled all in one common ruin.' (The Leech of Folkestone.)

That was written in 1840, and in the Preface he cannot refrain from adding in passing 'I can only add, that should business—pleasure is out of the question—ever call them into the neighbourhood of Folkestone . . .' We could quote other sources to support these views, and we must remember that the town had changed but little since Tudor times.

Other towns in Kent such as Margate, Ramsgate and Broadstairs had already developed into seaside resorts by the beginning of the nineteenth century, being caught up in the fashionable belief in the efficacy of drinking sea-water and sea-bathing as a cure for certain ailments. This was an offshoot from the idea of the value of mineral waters to be found at various

97

watering places such as Tunbridge Wells, Bath, Harrogate and
Scarborough. In fact quite early in the previous century the
existence of a mineral spring had been discovered at Foord
village, about a mile inland from the sea, and local residents
hoped that Foord might become a 'spa' like Tunbridge Wells.
But little or nothing was done to attract visitors or provide
suitable hotels if they came. This rather old-fashioned idea of
the inland spa was perhaps one reason for the late development of Folkestone as a resort—the promoters were on the
wrong track. For the real attraction of the seaside resort lay
in the amusements provided, the fashionable company and the
holiday atmosphere as well as the facilities for bathing in the
sea. Nothing of this existed in Folkestone—there was not even
a suitable hotel until 1843 when the South Eastern Railway
Company built the Pavilion Hotel.

HINTON'S VIEW

However, by 1830 a small beginning seems to have been
made according to Hinton's *Watering Places of Great Britain*.

> 'The bathing is good, the beach being clean, and the machines
> very neat. Were some marine residences and lodging houses
> erected on the cliff, on the entrance from Sandgate, there is
> little doubt, but that the number of bathing visitants would
> materially increase; a scantiness of characteristic accommoda-
> tion being a great inducement for marine visitors to search for
> it elsewhere . . . There is a sad paucity of Marine Lodging-
> houses, for, with the exception of two or three in the Sandgate
> Road, and here and there one or two in the vicinity of the
> churchyard, there are scarcely any.'

Mr. Hinton did his best for the town but he was obliged to
report a distinct disadvantage—'The pier which forms a good
promenade, is much frequented during the fine evenings; but
some sad eyesores on the town side surround the harbour,
comprising pig-styes, hovels and rookeries . . .'

LORD RADNOR TAKES THE INITIATIVE

Obviously the town needed a clean-up and a suitable area
where seaside residencies, lodging-houses and hotels could be
built. The first move came in 1825 when Lord Radnor secured
an Act of Parliament 'to enable building leases to be granted of
part of the settled estates of Jacob, Earl of Radnor in the

parishes of Folkestone and Cheriton in Kent', and he made available to local builders plots of land on long leases in the hope of stimulating building enterprise. Pigot's *Directory for 1826* notes: 'Lord Folkestone has contributed to the welfare of the town by the erection of neat houses in judicious situations, for the accommodation of visitors, who frequent Folkestone as a bathing place; and it promises ere long to become one of very fashionable resort.' Incidentally, it was at this time that Lord Radnor adopted the name of Folkestone as a second title for his family, and, moreoever, insisted that the old spelling of the name 'Folkstone' should be changed to 'Folkestone'. It seems that the Earl was determined to modernise and extend the town—in spite of apathy and derision; and during the rest of the century the judicious planning and control of the building by the Lords of the Manor have made the new Folkestone the gracious and spacious town it came to be. The later entries in Pigot's *Directories* reveal this fact. Thus in 1839 (before the railway came), Pigot reports: 'As yet there is a lack of lodging houses as compared with the demand, but great facility is afforded for the erection of new ones. A large extent of land, most eligibly situated, has been laid out by the Earl of Radnor for building purposes; and there are few places . . . that would better repay a well-directed building speculation'.

SIDNEY SMIRKE

But progress was extremely slow and nothing substantial seems to have been done for twenty years after the granting of the Act. Lord Radnor eventually decided to appoint a London architect, Mr. Sydney Smirke, to develop the estate, and in 1845 Smirke published a prospectus advertising the virtues of Folkestone and the great opportunities for building in the district:

'The genius of Steam, that has already effected so many extraordinary social changes in this country, has been peculiarly active here. A few years ago this small, secluded town lay unfrequented and little known . . . We find it now with a Railway direct from London, a capacious Harbour for large ships, a fine stone pier, and an Hotel with a hundred beds . . . This change in the character of Folkestone has been so wonderfully rapid, that we find it now almost without a house to receive a visitor.

A plan is laid down for the proposed arrangement of the building sites: their general aspect will be varied and irregular: it is intended specially to avoid the dull straight uniformity of most of our watering places: there will be no cheerless crowding together of close tenements, but plenty of air and space, and uninterrupted sea views will be preserved everywhere.'

But things were slow to move. A year later Smirke announced that sixteen acres had been let and that villas would shortly be built, but clearly he was not satisfied with the progress. In a new advertisement he praises Folkestone, forecasts a brilliant future for it, and denigrates Brighton and Dover . . . 'Brighton has become an overgrown suburb of London' and '. . . Dover, where, hemmed in on every side, it would be difficult to find a square foot of land, whereon another brick might be laid. The time is then near at hand when the palm must be ceded to this new favourite'. There is much more in the same vein, and it makes amusing reading now. Smirke was trying to promote the development of the land behind the harbour, from the Tram Road to the East Wear Bay, and he produced an elaborate plan showing nineteen plots for building, and even published a lithograph showing an imaginary view of the new estate as seen from the north-west. This was the 'Wear Bay Estate' in which 'all the houses will be built in conjunction with continuous covered ways in passages about 8 or 10 feet wide (roofed with glass) . . . so as to enable the residents to visit the covered Promenade, Aquarium, Reading Rooms, etc.' There were to be Concert Rooms, Bath Rooms, all connected by glass arcades, and sloping terraces and lawns for Croquet, Archery and other amusements. Unfortunately for Smirke this proved to be no more than a day dream for the idea never took on.

Smirke next produced a plan for the area extending from the West Cliff inland to the railway embankment, consisting of some twelve plots, including certain parts of the Leas, the lower Sandgate Road, and various plots along Cheriton Road and Back Lane. The plan was not well conceived and the net result seems to have been the erection of the three Albion Villas and two houses at the bottom of the Leas. The latter were later to be known as 1 and 2 The Leas, and were a private venture of Mr. R. W. Boarer, a former Mayor of the town, who foresaw the possibilities of the site. At the time the idea of building in an open field on the cliff was viewed with some amusement. Little other progress was made.

In 1849 Smirke produced a new and better plan, offering an attractive lay-out of the region west of Guildhall Street, stretching westward as far as a proposed new church (Christ Church), and lying between Sandgate Road and a new road called Bouverie Road East and West; it included a spacious square, Bouverie Square, and various side roads such as the West Cliff Gardens, West Terrace and Bouverie Place. Various plots on the Sandgate Road were also made available, so encouraging the town to grow westward. The plan offered a new lay-out of the Leas and it showed an 'Upper Private Road to Sandgate' which was to become the future Leas Promenade.

Smirke's third plan to develop the Sandgate Road area was more successful, and with the increase of visitors from 1849 onwards the new estate began to grow. In 1850 Smirke designed and supervised the building of Christ Church, and in 1852 the first National School, associated with the church, was built at the junction of Cheriton Road and Bouverie Road East. And so, at last, the West Cliff Estate began to take shape on the western side of the town. The Wear Bay Estate still hung fire.

Other developments now began in the lower part of the town. In the 50's several blocks of boarding houses were erected on the shore to the west of the Pavilion Hotel. These were very desirable lodgings promoted by Lord Radnor and designed to cater for seaside visitors. They ran out on a line westwards towards the Lower Sandgate Road, and before long a carriage drive was made in front of them, forming a 'Marine Parade'. Meanwhile, there was another proposal to build a new shopping centre in the Pent Valley behind the cluster of shops and dwellings between Pent Bridge and Kingsbridge. A 'Folkestone Tontine Building Company' was formed with the intention of making a road up the valley to meet Mill Lane, the stream being confined within a culvert which ran under the road. Previous to 1847 the shops in the valley bottom ended abruptly at the foot of High Street; and beyond was a green valley down which the stream ran until it disappeared under Pent Bridge. In the valley a track, still known as Mill Bay,

ran on the south side, and the only building on it was the little
Baptist Church, built on the site given by Mr. John Stace. A
contemporary description of the church and the valley in 1833
states:

> 'It was the only building within one hundred yards: the
> approach to it from the Dover Road (Mill Lane) was by a wide
> footpath or bridle road; it had in front a crescent shaped level
> meadow, bounded by the mill stream which now runs beneath
> Tontine Street. Northward of this again was a sloping bank
> now crossed by St. Michael's Street, but then covered by a
> flourishing orchard in which the thrush and the nightingale
> made melody. It was then as rural and sequestered a spot as
> any in the country.'

TONTINE STREET

It was up this sequestered valley that the new road was
begun in 1848; and it was intended to provide a modern
shopping centre for the town. Mr. Sidney Smirke, was employed
to design the street in Regency style, and something of its
original elegance can be perceived in the façade of the Claren-
don Hotel and in the upper storeys of the shops. Unfortunately
the town was hardly ready for this development, and only the
lower half of the street was built at first, many of the shops
remaining unoccupied for several years. But by the nineties
Tontine Street, as it was named, became the busiest shopping
centre in the town.

Another growing point in the late forties, before the Radnor
Estate got started, was the building of a street of residences
along Shellons Lane, and called at first 'Shellons Terrace'.
Originally the lane was bordered by fields on either side, and
where it met Cow Street (our Sandgate Road), stood the
King's Arms Hotel. Now private dwellings were erected along
one side, and a little later the street was renamed Guildhall
Street. Sandgate Road also began to have gentlemen's residences with gardens in front built along it, and contemporary
guide books refer to their 'rustic elegance'.

FOLKESTONE IMPROVEMENT ACT

The next major step in the development of the town came in
1855, when on 16th July the Council obtained an Act 'to
extend the limits of the Borough of Folkestone, to enable the

Corporation of the said Borough to construct a market house, to make certain new streets, and other improvements, and to pave, light, drain and otherwise improve the said Borough'. These were considerable powers which were over the next thirty years to make important changes in the older parts of the town. A certain amount of street-widening and clearance took place. In the harbour region the maze of dwellings bordering the lower stretch of the Pent stream was opened up and Harbour Street made, so that it was possible at last to drive down Tontine Street directly to the harbour. This stimulated the growth of shops here, and Tontine Street was extended to join up with Mill Lane, which was re-named Dover Road. The former Butcher Row (the top part of modern Rendezvous Street) was widened to 40 feet, and joined on to the lower section of Rendezvous Street, which itself was widened and continued along Grace Hill. Grigg's Lane, which ran from the Shakespeare Inn down to Copthall Gardens was built up and renamed 'Shellons Street'. And there was further development in the region of the 'Gun Tavern' where Smirke's new road, Bouverie Road East began.

THE TOWN HALL

Meanwhile the question of the Town Hall or Market House had to be settled. The old Guildhall, as we saw earlier, had been demolished in 1840, but it had ceased to be used for Council meetings after 1830. In that year the Cistern House, which stood on the site of the present Town Hall, was leased from Lord Radnor and altered for use as a Town Hall. Towards the end of 1850 the Corporation bought the Appollonian Hall in High Street and converted it into a Police Station and Sessions Hall. (This was the building which, as we saw, was erected by the Wesleyans as their Chapel in 1831. It is still there.) The Cistern House continued to be used until it was demolished in 1858. It was rather an unsightly building with a crenelated top and looked like a prison. Something more elegant was looked for, and what the town got after much dispute was described in Kelly's *Directory for 1870* as follows:

'The Town Hall was erected in 1860, on the site of the old one; it is in the Italian style, with plain rusticated ground floor and Corinthian columns, and entablature above, and with clock chamber over to form the central feature. The large hall is about 80 feet by 50 feet in size, and there are council, magistrates' and committee and other rooms in the building, with police station and market under.'

The reader may recognize this building as it still stands at the bottom of Sandgate Road, and it was regarded by many as a distinct ornament to the town at the time. It certainly was a great improvement upon what had preceded it, and moreover provided a large room for public meetings. No such room existed previously, and when Charles Dickens visited us in 1855 and gave a reading of *A Christmas Carol*, the best that could be found at the time was a carpenter's workshop in Dover Road. But now there was the possibility of the beginnings of a social and cultural life which was so sadly lacking in the town. Indeed, from its first opening the main hall was booked for Choral Society Concerts, Penny Readings, Christy's Minstrels, Amateur Theatricals and balls, all frequently repeated. We shall return to the question of entertainment later on.

All these developments and alterations took a considerable time, and the most congested parts of the town were altered first. But High Street, Dover Street, Broad Street and George Lane with their mixture of dwellings and shops were never widened and remained much as they were in the previous century; and most of them even now remain as a reminder of Folkestone's past history.

Meanwhile the Radnor Estate continued to grow westward. Sandgate Road was gradually built up as far as Christ Church, and side roads were opened such as West Cliff Gardens, West Terrace, and Bouverie Place leading to Bouverie Square. This last was greatly favoured on account of its pleasant private gardens and its Regency style balconies. On the south side of Sandgate Road several houses were combined to form Folkestone's second hotel, Bates's Hotel (the Esplanade), which has flourished under different names for over a century. It had a delightful view over the West Cliff Gardens and out to the sea. In a similar way the West Cliff Hotel was formed by the conversion of four large houses above Christ Church in the year 1857; subsequently it was enlarged and renamed the Majestic Hotel.

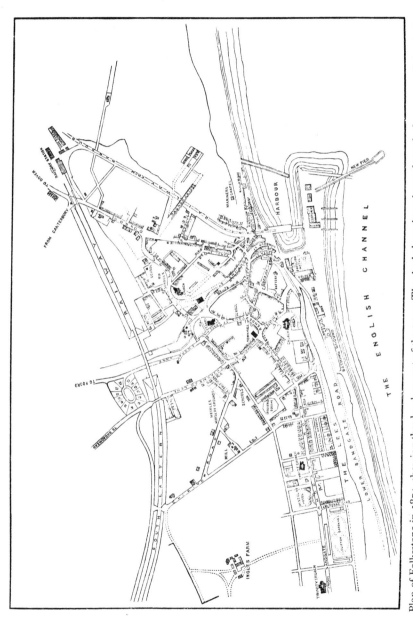

Plan of Folkestone in 1874, showing the development of the town. The shaded portions show where the houses were being built. (From Mackie's *Handbook of Folkestone for Visitors*, 1874.)

GROWTH OF THE TOWN

While the fashionable Radnor Estate continued to grow, it is surprising to see how slowly the town itself responded to the situation. There was a little building along the line of the railway, including Darlington Street, Viaduct Villas and opposite the Junction Station, soon after the arrival of the railway. By 1865 a few houses appeared in Victoria Grove, in Shellons Street, in Dover Road above St. Michael's Church, and in London Street. Shortly before 1848 the Radnor Bridge had been constructed over the Harbour Branch line to facilitate the development of the Wear Bay Estate, but by 1874 only a few new dwellings had been erected, such as East Cliff, Waterloo Terrace and Trafalgar Terrace. By 1874 houses appeared along Broadmead Lane, at the junction of Cheriton Road and Bouverie Road East, and in the upper stretch of Dover Road above St. Mary's National Schools, which were erected in 1855. One or two isolated villas were built along the Cheriton Road towards the Cheriton Arch; however the windmill in the future Cheriton Gardens still dominated the fields of Ingles Farm. It was not until the eighties that building began to the north and east of the town to provide accommodation for the artisan classes, the servants, tradesmen, shop-assistants and labourers. It would be tedious to describe all these developments, but it is interesting to note how the railway embankment seemed to restrict building in this direction, the only developments being along Foord Road after the transfer of the Gas Works there in 1866, and along the Canterbury Road by the Junction Station.

SERVICES

We must retrace our steps now to consider the supply of the services and amenities necessary to a growing modern town. What it needed was a good water supply and a system of sanitation. At the beginning of the century Folkestone had neither. From what we have said about the dirty state of the streets and the insanitary habits of the inhabitants it will be obvious that the town had no sewage disposal arrangements. There was only a series of brick drains in a few of the streets. In 1797 there was a report of one drain that emptied its contents over the Bayle cliff. This must have been an eyesore

PLATE 25. Folkestone Bathing Establishment, as originally built, *c.* 1870. (Folkestone Museum.)

PLATE 26. Fagg's Patent Bathing Carriage, with safety cage. (Folkestone Museum.)

PLATE 27. Victoria Pier. Regatta Day. Note the Switchback Railway in the foreground. (Folkestone Museum.)

PLATE 28. View from Pier of foreshore and Regatta crowds. (Folkestone Museum.)

PLATE 29. Colliers unloading on west quay, *c.* 1900. (Folkestone Museum.)

PLATE 30. Man carrying coals to the coal carts on the quay. A frequent scene in the old days. (Folkestone Museum.)

PLATE 31. The National Art Treasures Exhibition Building. Later the Pleasure Gardens Theatre. (Folkestone Museum.)

PLATE 32. Fashion Parade on the Leas on Sundays. A typical Edwardian scene. (Folkestone Museum.)

and a discouragement to bathers. The brick drains running down High Street and Dover Street were reported in 1815 to be ill-constructed, and they emptied into the Pent stream, and the sewage collected in the harbour. In 1866 the Corporation adopted a scheme of drainage proposed by Sir Joseph Bazalgette, at a cost of £3,500; there was some improvement, but Folkestone's drains got a very bad reputation, and even as late as 1875, Lord Robert Montague, a local resident, reported on the foul drains to the House of Commons. His report got into the press; there was great local indignation, and protest meetings were held in the Town Hall. Folkestone people did not mind the bad drains so much as the bad publicity they brought—it does not seem to have occurred to them that Sir Robert was right, and that the frequent epidemics of typhoid were due to the lack of sanitation. The South Eastern Railway was concerned since the sewage went into their harbour; so, eventually, the Railway Company and the local Sanitary Authority jointly constructed a new sewer carrying the sewage from the Pent stream eastward under the Stade and out into the sea by the East Sands.

WATER

Obviously a water-borne sanitation system could not be installed until a satisfactory water supply had been provided. For centuries the people living on the Bayle had relied on St. Eanswythe's stream which ran all the way from a point just west of Castle Hill to the town, ultimately running along the north side of Guildhall Street and filling the Bayle Pond. It was known as the Town Dyke and there were various dipping points along its route. Those living in the Pent valley relied on the springs issuing below Spring Terrace, where a town pump was installed. These were inadequate for a seaside town and insufficient for flushing the drains. In 1848 the Folkestone Water Company was formed, and they bought up the Cherry Gardens west of Castle Hill, with its natural springs and pond. The Cherry Gardens had long been a favourite resort for picnics, and for Folkestone people to visit on summer evenings. Soon afterwards it was closed to the public, and the clear waters used to provide a piped supply from 1850 onwards. The Company also bought the water rights in the Bradstone area

8

from Mr. Stace; and the Company still supplies the town and a large district round.

GAS

In 1842 a supply of gas was provided, largely through the efforts of the Town Clerk, Mr. R. T. Brockman. This was another example of the progress of the town due to the efforts of one citizen; otherwise, this amenity might have been much delayed. He formed a Company with a capital of £2,500 and a Gas Works was erected in 1841, on the Lower Sandgate Road, just west of the Pavilion Hotel, where it was convenient to carry the sea-borne coal. The first supply was made on 29th December, 1842, when there were sixty consumers and thirty street lamps. Here was a great innovation—the introduction of street lighting.

Owing to the expansion of the town in the late 50's and 60's there was a great demand for further supplies of gas—much greater than the little seaside works could provide. Growth on this site was restricted, so a fresh site was sought in Foord Road. The little village of Foord was still isolated from the rest of the town, and the only way to it was via Rendezvous Street and Grace Hill and so by Foord Lane. A site was eventually secured just beyond the viaduct, although it was already occupied by a charming estate of Swiss-style chalets known as Viaduct Villas; these had to be demolished gradually to make way for the new Gas Works. The Folkestone Gas Act of 1865 established a new Company and a larger Gas Works was erected, with its huge retorts and gasholders. The result may be imagined. The idyllic valley of Foord, already invaded by the railway, became a built up area. A further difficulty was encountered. The heavy demand for coal, brought up in horse-drawn carts from the colliers in the harbour, forced the building of a road direct from the top of Tontine Street to the middle of Foord Road. Previously, the coal carts had to haul the coal up Mill Lane to Rendezvous Street, turn right at the Wesleyan Church, and then negotiate the slope down Grace Hill to the works. So a new road had to be made joining the top of Tontine Street to the middle section of Foord Road, thus avoiding part of the steep hill. The new road came to be known as the 'Milky Way' because the coal carts returning to the harbour, carried chalk as ballast for the ships; and the spill from them produced a white dust in summer and a muddy porridge in winter.

In 1875 further expansion was needed, and a large new gas-holder holding 200,000 cu. ft. of gas was built on the site. The occasion was marked by a champagne lunch for 250 guests held inside the gas-holder in December, 1875; and the interior was illuminated with gas jets and decorated with greenery. (In 1956 the holders became gas storers for Dover Gas, and the local retorts were demolished in 1958).

ELECTRICITY

Electricity, of course, came much later than the gas. The Folkestone Electricity Supply Company was founded in 1897, and electricity works were erected at Morehall in 1898. There had been a great deal of opposition to the coming of electricity, and in 1894 protest meetings were held in the Town Hall against the use of electric lighting in the streets. The first consumer was the West Cliff Hotel in May, 1898, but several hotels already generated their own supplies, including the Pavilion, Wampach's and the Metropole, before the public supply was started. To begin with there were eighty consumers and twenty-four electric arc lamps for street lighting. (Since 1960 the Morehall works have become a sub-station for transmitting current to other places.) Gradually electricity was adopted for lighting shops and places of entertainment, and eventually private houses. Today electricity has completely replaced gas for street lighting, there being over 3,000 street lamps.

So far we have been considering some of the fundamental services which a modern town needed to cope with expanding demands, and to serve a seasonal influx of visitors. Some idea of the problem will be understood when we realize that the resident population of the town grew from 4,000 in 1800 to 30,500 in 1900. We will now consider the amenities which the town offered to the visitor.

CHAPTER NINE

SEASIDE PLEASURES, AMENITIES
AND AMUSEMENTS

GOOD facilities and accommodation for bathing are the first essentials for a seaside resort. The earliest indications of such facilities at Folkestone are to be found in an advertisement in the *Kentish Gazette* for 6th July, 1787, the advertisement being repeated the next year in May, 1788. It read that there are 'two elegant bathing machines genteely fitted and ready for the recreation of gentlemen and ladies'. This was a very humble beginning, but it does not appear to have been supported very much as we hear nothing more until 24th June, 1795, when another advertisement appeared in the *Kentish Gazette*, as follows: 'The public is informed that the bathing machines will be regularly attended every day during the season: and for the accommodation of those who drink sea water the purest will be procured every morning and placed in the waiting house on the Parade.' The reference to drinking sea water reminds us that bathing was still considered as a medical treatment for certain complaints rather than as a recreation and an amusement. This might have been the beginning of the development of the town as a watering place, but it does not appear to have been taken up, owing to the indifference of the natives and the lack of suitable accommodation. The idea that a bathing place might become a pleasure resort had not arrived. Indeed, until the first harbour pier had been built, so causing a foreshore to build up to the west of it, there were few bathing machines. On the other hand we learn from a *Guide to All the Watering Places* (1806):

'Besides the bathing-machines, which are like those of other places, here are bathing-rooms in Pent Street, near the sea, under the direction of Mr. Elgar, and in Dover-Street others conducted by Mr. Gill, a medical practitioner of respectability. This gentleman has also erected warm salt-water baths, at a considerable expense: and the situation of his house and bathing rooms is remarkably pleasant and salubrious.'

This account shows how the medical aspect of sea-bathing persisted for some years and possibly delayed the development of the town as a pleasure resort. We have already seen how the Chalybeate spring at Foord with its sham ruin indicated the trend of ideas at the time.

The gradual build-up of the sand and shingle favoured the use of machines for a time. 'The gentle declivity of the shore, and being well sheltered from the wind, renders the bathing not only safe, but pleasant in any state of the wind or tide.' But after a few years a difficulty arose over their use. In the early years the shore was sandy and it was convenient for a horse to draw the machines to the water's edge. But gradually a considerable bank of shingle accumulated in steep ridges and covered the sand, thus making it difficult to control the machine. An early sketch of a Folkestone bathing machine (1844) shows it with very wide-rimmed wagon wheels which were adopted to prevent it from sinking too far into the shingle. But the steeply shelving shore made bathing dangerous to all but confident swimmers.

THE BATHING ESTABLISHMENT

To overcome this difficulty and to offer bathing facilities at all seasons the Folkestone Bathing Establishment was built in 1868 on the Lower Sandgate Road. This building, erected in the Italian style to match several other local buildings, provided much more than a heated sea-water swimming bath. To quote a contemporary account:

'On the lower tier is a large swimming and plunge bath, and also every description of medicated and 'invalid' baths: the first floor is devoted to a series of warm and cold baths, which are all fitted in the most excellent style: . . . and the upper tier, which has an entrance from the cliff (the house being built on the slope of the hill), is set apart from the subscription and assembly rooms, which are furnished in the same manner, and possess all the characteristics of the best London clubs, comprising reading, billiard, and refreshment rooms, besides the large saloon, which is used for the balls and concerts that take place periodically, and at other times as a lounge for the subscribers.'

This was something more grand and fashionable than anything Folkestone had seen before, and it served to attract well-to-do visitors to the new hotels on the Leas. The bathing machines still continued in use for those who preferred the freshness and the hazards of the sea. To quote again:

> 'On a hot summer's day Folkestone beach is like a fair—and a very gay one too—with the numbers of ladies, gentlemen and children waiting for their turn to bathe, and listlessly casting pebbles in the sea, or whiling away the time with novels.'

FAGG'S BATHING CARRIAGE

So in the 1870's Folkestone took its place among the popular bathing resorts of Kent—with this difference, that it became the resort of the more fashionable and wealthy as more and more high quality boarding houses were built and as entertainments of a refined and discreet type were provided. As time went on it became impracticable to draw the cumbersome machines up and down the steep shelving beach. A solution was provided by the ingenuity of a local man, a Mr. Fagg, who invented the 'Fagg's Patent Bathing Carriage'. This consisted of a long narrow cabin like a small railway carriage, divided into some twenty compartments inside. It was mounted on a sloping undercarriage which ran on wheels along an elevated railway track. It could be hoisted up or down the track according to the state of the tide; and at the seaward end there was a large boom, attached to which was fixed a large rope cage for the protection of non-swimmers. There were two of these machines—one for men and the other for women—and they remained in use for many years. Later they were replaced by a large enclosure of fixed bathing cabins, divided into two for the sexes. Mixed bathing was permitted only from private tents erected on the western beach.

One of the problems of the seaside resort in the early years was to provide adequate amusement for the visitor after he had taken his morning dip. Folkestone was well provided with interesting walks. Charles Dickens, who was an energetic walker, testified to his enjoyment of the country round the town; he went on long walks along the shore to neighbouring towns, and inland over the North Downs and along the lanes to various country villages. But for those who were less energetic there were agreeable walks along the Lower Sandgate Road, which had been made by Lord Radnor many years before. In 1876 the Undercliff was extensively developed as a pleasure ground and secluded promenade. There were shrubberies, a series of gardens with alcoves and arbours, and winding pathways. Similarly, the spacious promenade above on the Leas was laid out in the nineties with lawns, shelters and bandstands. The feeling of elevation as one looked out to sea, the interest of watching the shipping of all kinds passing through the Straits, and the attraction of promenading—of seeing and being seen—all provided an unusual feature of the Folkestone scene. To this must be added the advantages offered by the two lifts which conveyed the visitor up or down the cliff with a minimum of trouble. The first lift was installed in 1885 just prior to the building of the Victoria Pier; the western lift was installed particularly for the guests of the Metropole Hotel in 1904; and a third, the Sandgate lift, was made in 1893.

VICTORIA PIER

The pleasure pier was a fashionable feature of most seaside resorts in the late nineteenth century, and Folkestone's Victoria Pier was formally opened on 21st July, 1888. It was of a pleasing design, 680 feet in length with embayed recesses and a Concert Pavilion at the end. Here concerts and band performances were given, and musicians of international reputation were engaged from London. This was an added attraction to those visitors who enjoyed good music. And from the pier deck, interesting views could be had of the Lower Sandgate Road and the beach. An additional feature was the ornamental gardens at the main entrance, with shrubs, flowers, parterres and ornamental kiosks illuminated at night. The pier proved to be really popular, over 7,000 people passing through the turnstiles during the first day, and at one time there was a proposal to extend the pier to double its length.

SHIPPING

The Harbour and the South Eastern Pier also offered considerable interest to visitors. There were always the cross-channel boats to be watched, arriving or departing, the unloading of colliers in the inner harbour, and the busy scenes of the fishing quarter. One observer, writing in 1870, describes the view out to sea as follows. It must be remembered that he was writing in the days when sail still predominated:

'The seaside, too, has other and more popular attractions than the fishermen. The number of ships of all sizes, kinds and countries, that are constantly going up and down the channel, are endless sources of amusement and delight, while the nearness with which they approach the shore, render these scenes so much more interesting than at Hastings, Brighton, and other places along the coast, where the shipping is only seen in the offing, and nothing larger than a fishing-boat ever approaches the land. Here the leviathan three-decker comes within so short a distance of our pier that old shipmate captains recognise each other, and the music of the band and the boatswain's whistle are distinctly heard; colliers and schooners bring up in our bays, and fleets of vessels often "stand" so close in that we can read the painted letters on their sides or sterns as they "tack" out to sea again. Steamers, pilot-boats and cruisers, merchant-vessels and traders, from the great East Indiaman or Australian clipper, to the smaller vessel bound to Cape Castle and the African Coast, or some little "fruiter" for the Mediterranean, are all mingled together on the blue water.

After a long easterly or westerly wind, when the vessels, which have been held in check for some days in the Downs, or behind Dungeness, take the first breath of a favourable change, the sight of such numbers of ships all in motion at once is truly magnificent. On these occasions upwards of three hundred "sail" may be frequently counted.'

These interesting sights and the delightful background of farms, fields and hills gave Folkestone an undoubted advantage. Its scenic attractions, with the old church on the West Cliff and the fishing town below, made it a favourite subject for artists at all periods, and the appearance of the town in its various stages of growth is well represented in engravings, water colours and photographs.

BANDS

The provision of music appears to have been a peculiar concern of the town. We must remember that in the nineteenth century there was a dearth of music other than that provided by itinerant singers. There were no gramophones, radios or television to fill the air with sound. All music had to be live music, and apart from the occasional performance of a military band from Shorncliffe Camp, little was heard. An amusing sidelight on the question may be seen in a set of verses published in a local newspaper in February, 1853 (Appendix 3). Here the author notes the readiness with which the Mayor and local citizens subscribed to a fund for engaging a French band for the summer, but how reluctant they were to pay the church rates for the upkeep of the Parish Church.

There were other private sources of music, often supplied by the hotels for their guests. One of these was the West Cliff Hotel 'in the spacious grounds behind which fashion is wont to disport itself, at the cost of a shilling, when the weather is propitious, to the strains of a military band, amid the sub-dued glare of a myriad of Japanese or Badoura lanterns'.

BANDSTANDS

But it was not until 1893 that the Corporation undertook to provide facilities for public concerts. The Folkestone Corpo-ration Act (1893) gave consent to erect bandstands. The first appears to have been built in 1893 in the Marine Gardens which had been extensively laid out and planted at the same time. The second was erected on the Leas opposite Clifton Gardens in 1895—the only one still standing. The third came about more by accident than by design. The Metropole Hotel was built at the west end of the Leas in 1897 in a setting of gardens, lawns and tennis courts. In the grounds between the wings of the hotel a bandstand was erected for the delectation of guests. Unfortunately the sounds reverberated from the walls and disturbed them. So the proprietors of the hotel (Gordon Hotels Ltd.) gave the bandstand to the Corporation, who erected it on the West Leas in front of the hotel in 1902. There it was much appreciated and fashionable crowds sat on chairs round the bandstand to listen to A. Newmann's 'Red Hungarian Band' or, later, Herr Worm's 'Blue Viennese Band'.

At the end of the century a private body, the 'Folkestone Amusements Association' was formed to organize and supply musical entertainments for visitors. They were responsible for the establishment of the Leas Shelter (1894), a concert room to which military bands could repair in wet weather. A con-temporary account describes it thus:

'High up on the cliff-face, almost opposite Castle Hill Avenue, and reached by sloping pathways and steps from either the

Leas or the Lower Sandgate Road, is perched a rustic building known as the Leas Shelter. An open balcony, *a la Suisse*, with a spacious platform provides seating accommodation and the finest view in the town for some scores of loungers; while behind is a large hall, in which an orchestra plays daily.'

This building with its spacious balcony proved to be very popular, as it was sheltered from the sometimes boisterous winds and was delightfully warm at all seasons. Visitors read their papers and novels under the glass canopy and listened to the light music of the band. But this was not the end of the tale of amusements provided by the enterprising citizens of the town, who in those days were willing to invest their money in local concerns.

PLEASURE GARDENS THEATRE

In 1886 the Folkestone Art Treasures Exhibition Company was formed. Its object was to bring to the town specimens of the best painting and sculpture for exhibition. A large exhibition hall was built with a glass roof and spacious galleries, somewhat after the style of the Crystal Palace. To attract visitors from neighbouring towns a special railway line was run from Shorncliffe Station to the building, which was set in extensive ornamental grounds. The project did not obtain the expected support, and closed after only five months. Two years later it changed hands and became the property of the 'Folkestone Exhibition Palace Company'. Soon after the name was changed again to the 'Pleasure Gardens Company' the emphasis being on recreation rather than art. The grounds of sixteen acres were laid out for tennis, hockey, croquet and skating, and there was a rustic bandstand. Military displays and tournaments were a popular attraction. The Exhibition building was converted into a theatre to seat 1,000 people, and opened in 1888 as the Exhibition Palace Theatre. It was later called the Pleasure Gardens Theatre and for many years a weekly programme of plays, opera, Shakespearean productions, romantic comedies, revues and musical shows were presented all the year round. In its hey-day it was a great asset to the town, and being situated in the west end, it provided superior entertainment for wealthy residents.

LEAS PAVILION

One other source of popular entertainment was added at the beginning of the next century. In 1902 a superior 'Tea Room' was opened on the Leas and known as the Leas Pavilion. To begin with, music was supplied by a ladies' string trio—a distinct novelty at the time. It became so popular that vocal solos were added as an attraction, and before long a stage with proscenium curtains was installed and Concert Parties gave shows twice each day, and the tea-drinking took a subordinate place. Concert Parties were a new development of the day— a more elegant version of the Pierrots on the beach. The concerts at the Leas Pavilion became a permanent feature of the Folkestone scene, and 'The Gypsies and their Jester' were a concert troupe whose programmes are still remembered. In between the wars the management turned to repertory.

Reference to the Pierrots recalls the fact that temporary booths were erected on the beach beside the Marine Gardens and that for many seasons a troupe of male singers known as 'Cardow's Cadets' sang sentimental ballads and comic songs, somewhat after the style of the Nigger Minstrels.

THE SWITCHBACK

The beach also provided other attractions apart from bathing. In 1891 a lease of the foreshore just west of the Victoria Pier was granted for the erection of a 'Switchback Railway'. This was a wooden structure running parallel with the shore, with a railway track starting from a platform some 40 feet high. Along the track a six-seater trolley ran on an undulating course with steep dips and rises which were intended to excite and alarm the passenger. It was the forerunner of all the Great Racers dear to seaside resorts of a later date. It was intended to provide amusement for the ordinary holiday maker, but it was found that Prime Ministers and even Princesses were addicted to it.

Other features of the Folkestone seashore were the inevitable Camera Obscura, a Rowing Club, a Life Boat Station, and the vendors of 'Hokey-Pokey, Penny a Lump'. There were also trips along the coast to Ramsgate in the South Eastern Paddle Steamers, trips round the bay in a sailing yacht, fishing from a rowing boat or from the pier, and the fascinating search for winkles and crabs among the rocks at low tide.

HOVELLERS

After all these sophisticated amusements it is refreshing to return to a feature of the Folkestone shore of the sixties and seventies, as described by a contemporary:

> 'Long galleys lie on the shore, and lots of little varnished boats, with bright red and white flags; the former are service boats, the latter playthings for visitors. They do well enough for a calm day, but are scarcely to be trusted in the slightest breeze unless under the management of a skilful sailor.
>
> The galleys belong to sailors of an amphibious character, called 'hovellers" whose principal occupation consists in pacing up and down a small portion of the shore with a telescope, which they turn attentively every now and then on the shipping. If a ship want fresh meat or vegetables, or has a passenger to put ashore, or letters, or is in any want or distress, or a collier needs a pilot to bring her into port, one (or more) of the galleys is put off and the best bargain made, in which, as the hovellers generally have their own way, the advantage is usually on their side. When the crews of two or three boats discover a signal at some little distance from the galleys, a race takes place, and the nimblest of foot claims the prize, and his boat is immediately launched.'

The hoveller is now a thing of the past and his place taken by the Trinity Pilot in his swift motor launch—still a fascinating sight—but the hovellers racing out to the multitude of sailing vessels of the mid-nineteenth century must have provided a fund of interest.

RADNOR PARK

As the town grew further inland past the railway embankment, which had hitherto tended to restrict the northward development, Lord Radnor gave to the town a large recreation ground of some 16 acres at a peppercorn rent. The area was opened to the public in 1885 and called 'Radnor Park'; and it was laid out with trees, flower-beds and a bowling green in the upper section. The lower part provided two ornamental ponds, the upper one being fed with water from St. Eanswyth's stream; and the lower one, designed for model yachts, emptied into the Pent stream valley, which was provided with paths, rustic seats, a waterfall and shelters. One feature was the famous 'crooked oak' which leaned over the stream. The park has been an adornment to the town ever since, and needless to say it encouraged still more building in the area, particularly of large and ornate houses for the wealthy.

A NEW STATION

With the growth of the town on the north and west there was a demand for a new station in a more convenient place than the earlier ones. The Junction Station was too far to the east, and the Harbour Station too far south. In 1884 the South Eastern Railway was persuaded to supply one close to the point where Cheriton Road went under the railway line, and they called it 'Cheriton Arch', because of the rounded arch in the embankment, like the present Darlington Arch. But visitors failed to connect the name with Folkestone and frequently went on to the Junction Station. So in 1887 the name was changed to 'Radnor Park Station'; but the result was just as confusing, and visitors still alighted at the Junction. At last, in 1895, it was renamed 'Folkestone Central' and it has remained the principal station ever since.

FASHIONABLE FOLKESTONE

We have had occasion to mention the benevolent interest which the Radnor family took in the development of the town; they also strove to give it a certain cachet of wealth and exclusiveness which was very noticeable at the end of the nineteenth century. An observer at the time writes:

'By 1901 Folkestone had become the most aristocratic seaside resort in the country, though perhaps it was nearly equalled by Eastbourne'. Another says: 'Lord Radnor, who owned (and still owns) the Leas, had his own policeman, blue uniform, gold-braided peak cap, to patrol the promenade with measured, stately tread. His short cane was a ready corrective to many mischief-bent small boys'. Another contemporary writes with due unction:

> 'Folkestone, since it became a watering place, has always retained a hold on the more moneyed of those who go down to the sea in summer. It does not lay itself out to attract the ephemeral tripper. It even holds itself aloof from the sea,

caters for a class that does not sit on the beach, a class that regards the sea with the platonic liking that it confers on personages both estimable and *ennuyant*. The air is not impregnated with brine, does not unduly quicken, does not render one embarrassingly boisterous. Hence its attractions for legislators who shun places more marine . . . Thus on the Leas on a Sunday one may see the Distinguished and the Wealthy rub shoulders in pleasant contiguity, instinct with the satisfactory knowledge that they have achieved their weekly devotions and that a good dinner awaits a good appetite. The edges of prayer-books gleam along the smooth grass, the sun shines, the dresses rustle discreetly, the voices simulate the murmur of the sea. The sea itself keeps at a respectful distance, acts as a good servant, silently supplying the necessary ozone . . . This is the real philosophy of a Folkestone season. This is the town's justification, its apologia pro vita sua.'

Of course this was aristocratic west end Folkestone, with its bath chairs for elderly ladies and invalids, its broughams with high-stepping horses and Dalmatians, its nannies and butlers and ushers. There was a more robust Folkestone down by the harbour, in the Marine Gardens, along South Street, Harbour Street and Tontine Street with its pubs and cheap restaurants. And there was still another Folkestone which one finds so vividly described in *Kipps*. And beyond all these there was the homely, salty life of the fishing quarter. But the difference between the first group and the others was carefully preserved by the weekly publication of a 'Visitors' List', giving the names of all the titled and distinguished visitors to the town and their Folkestone addresses. And Pike's local directories always divided the residents into two categories—'Court' and 'general'. Shades of Chester-Coote!

CHAPTER TEN

SOCIAL, RELIGIOUS AND EDUCATIONAL DEVELOPMENTS

W E return once more to the beginning of the nineteenth century to trace various other aspects of the town's development. From what we have said in Chapter VI of the backward state of the town before 1840 there was little likelihood of cultural activity either for natives or for visitors. A small guide book of 1810 says this of Folkestone:

> 'The amusements of this place are but few when compared to some of its neighbours. Here is, however, a small theatre, which is only occupied in the winter, and an assembly room called the Apollo. The Circulating Library, kept by Roden, however, may be considered one of the principal amusements. The library is regularly furnished with the London and provincial newspapers, magazines and other periodical publications, and it is well supplied with new books. And this Repository forms a most agreeable lounge every Tuesday and Friday evening during the season, and is well attended.'

This notice makes the best of the situation, and very probably Roden's was patronized by the professional classes who were few in number. Many of the inhabitants could not read at all, and their ignorance and illiteracy were well known, and gave rise to the comic ballad, probably written by a Dover man, called 'The Folkestone Fiery Serpent'. This amusing poem deserves to be read as it gives something of the atmosphere of the time—though somewhat exaggerated. The reference in the passage above to the 'season' is wishful thinking as even twenty years later the writers of guide books say that the place 'promises ere long to become a watering place'—but it took another forty years to do it. The Apollo Assembly room was a small room in Queen's Place, and was certainly not large enough for a public meeting of any size.

LIBRARIES AND NEWSPAPERS

Visitors to the seaside would expect to find a Circulating Library, and Roden's must have been one of the earliest. As the century progressed more stationers, booksellers and printers set up, most of them in the High Street which for many years remained the shopping centre. Edmund Creed opened in 1844 and Henry Stock was in business in 1847. John English was one of the most active, and lasted the longest. He collaborated with Stock to produce Folkestone's first newspaper in 1855. Joseph Riley also established himself in the High Street, and proclaimed that he had 'the largest library in the town'. All of these sold the usual stationers' goods, Berlin wools and an interesting range of engravings of the town. As the population grew various firms ventured on publishing a local newspaper. We have mentioned Stock and English's paper, the *Folkestone Chronicle* which ran from 1855 to 1886. The *Folkestone Observer* ran from 1861 to 1892; the *Express* (another of English's ventures) lasted the longest, from 1868 to 1940; and the *Folkestone News* ran from 1877 to 1890. In the seventies there were no fewer than seven local papers! One other publication which deserves mention was Holbein's *Visitors' List* (1885-1897) which, in addition to local news, announced the arrival of distinguished visitors. Both Stock and English published guides to Folkestone and district. The *Folkestone Herald* did not appear until 1890.

There was also an increasing demand from the residents as the years passed for reading matter of an informative kind. In 1845 the Harveian Literary Institution was formed, its aims being the diffusion of useful knowledge, the founding of a library, the arranging of a programme of lectures on literary and scientific subjects and the establishment of a museum of local natural history. This society established its premises in the old Theatre on the Bayle, but it had a chequered existence owing to its high subscription, and it came to an end in 1859. However it did start the idea of a public library and museum service. Another society, The Working Men's Educational Union, formed in 1853 with a lower subscription achieved a greater popularity and eventually took over the premises of the Harveian Literary Institution. In 1869 it extended the premises to include a new reading room, a library and committee room, and adopted the new name of the 'Harveian Institute'. The Institute's objects were much the same as those of the Harveian Literary Institution's, but they included

meetings of a more entertaining type. Latterly they too found
difficulty in maintaining their membership, and by 1876 their
funds were running out.

PUBLIC LIBRARY AND MUSEUM

Meanwhile, in 1868 the 'Folkestone Natural History Society'
was formed, one of its objects being the formation of a museum
to house a valuable collection of fossils which had been given
to the town. The Corporation made available to the Society a
room at the Sessions Hall in the High Street, provided that they
maintained it and exhibited the collection to the public. The
growth of the collections and the need for better premises
caused the Society to join forces with the Folkestone School of
Science in persuading the Corporation to adopt the Public
Libraries and Museums Acts. After considerable argument in
the Council this was done in May, 1878. In August, 1878, the
Harveian Institute offered to make over to the Council the
lease of its premises and its library for the purpose of the
Public Libraries Acts, and the offer was accepted. The premises
were further enlarged and the new library was opened in
January, 1879. So Folkestone got its first public library through
the initiative of several local societies, and it proved to be such a
success that it soon needed a larger building. This was provided
in 1888 when the present Public Library and Museum in
Grace Hill was opened by Sir Edward Watkin, the local
Member of Parliament. The museum collections and the
library were now under one roof, and the town has enjoyed
ever since one of the best libraries in Kent, and there are now
three branch libraries as well. (As a measure of the library's
success we may quote the number of books issued in various
years: in 1889 it was 16,335; in 1900 it was 57,811; and in
1970–71 it was 795,955.) The Library also possesses much
valuable material in its local history collection.

THE THEATRE

We have quoted a reference to a small theatre in our opening
paragraph. This was a small building on the Bayle, later used
by the Harveian Institute. It was advertised in 1774 as the
'New Theatre' and Mrs. Sarah Baker's troupe, the 'Sadler's

9

Wells Company' performed for two months there in 1775, performing as many as twenty-two different plays. A description of the building dating from 1800 describes it as a tarred weatherboarded structure with a roof like an upturned boat. There were backless benches in the pit and two boxes on the stage. The gallery was reached by a wooden ladder over the stage. It was still in use in 1855 as Dickens tells us in his essay *Out of the Season*. The town had to wait until 1888 before it got a modern theatre—the Exhibition Palace Theatre which we have already described.

Dickens provides us with a picture of Folkestone amusements in the mid-century:

'We are not strong in other public amusements. We have a Literary and Scientific Institution, and we have a Workingmen's Institution—may it hold many gipsy holidays in summer fields, with the kettle boiling, the band of music playing, and the people dancing; and may I be on the hillside, looking on with pleasure at a wholesome sight too rare in England!—and we have two or three churches, and more chapels than I have yet added up. But public amusements are scarce with us. If a poor theatrical manager comes with his company to give us, in a loft, *Mary Bax* or the *Murder on the Sandhills*, we don't much care for him—starve him out in fact. We take more kindly to waxworks, especially if it moves . . . Cooke's Circus gives us only a night in passing through. Nor does the travelling menagerie think us worth a longer visit.'

Apart from the entertainments mentioned by Dickens an occasional visit from Wombwell's Circus, and various itinerant musicians with their barrel organs and dancing bears, there was little to amuse the visitor at this time. It is not surprising that the town authorities took steps to supply better fare as the seaside resort grew.

THE PARISH CHURCH

The provision of churches of various denominations and the condition of the Parish Church now occupied the attention of religious bodies in the town. The Parish Church had suffered considerably from dilapidation and neglect during the eighteenth century. In 1705 it had been damaged in a great storm which demolished two bays at the west end. Fearing that the church might slip down the cliff in the next landslide, the parishioners petitioned the Archbishop to allow them to do the minimum repairs, and so a make-shift west end resembling a farmhouse was erected as a temporary measure. The church had been given a low ceiling and the arrangement of box-pews and galleries which shut out the light all produced a dull and depressing effect. The churchyard was overfull, and was closed to further interments in 1856, a new cemetery being provided on the Cheriton Road.

The restoration of the church began in 1859 under the supervision of the architect, R. C. Hussey. The whole of the building west of the tower was taken down and re-erected, adding 40 feet in length, and increasing the width of the side aisles as well as the size of the north transept, thus providing an increase of 200 sittings. The work was done in the early lancet style to match the architecture of the east end. The unsightly galleries which disfigured the old church were removed, a small one being placed at the west end, called the Pavilion gallery, and another over the new entrance opened in the north transept. In 1862 the church paths were widened and paved, the churchyard walls rebuilt, and the church itself enclosed in iron railings. The inspirer of this renovation was the new vicar, Rev. Matthew Woodward, who transformed the church and its services during his vicariate.

The restoration of the chancel was carried out in 1869 through the generosity of Lord Radnor. The flat ceiling of lath and plaster which had for many years disfigured the building was removed, to reveal the original rafters of the roof. The oval vesica window which had so long been hidden was restored, and the church was cleared of obstructions. The old organ which formerly stood in the north transept was replaced by a new one which was put in the south transept, where it is now. Stained glass was put into the chancel windows. Altogether the church must have presented in the seventies, a far better appearance than it had for centuries. Unfortunately the generosity of visitors and local benefactors tended to furnish the church with too much decoration. An alabaster reredos was added and the chaste lancet windows of the west end were replaced by a large decorated stained glass window in memory of Dr. William Harvey. These and a large number of wall paintings have a rather overpowering effect.

NEW CHURCHES

The growth of the town westward caused Lord Radnor to build a new church in the west end for the convenience of visitors. This was Christ Church in Sandgate Road, built in 1850, close to the West Cliff Hotel. Although small at first, it had to be enlarged several times and was eventually given a clock tower. The continued growth westward necessitated another new church, and in 1868 Lord Radnor erected Holy Trinity Church in Sandgate Road. At this time Earls Avenue, Castle Hill Avenue and Bouverie Road West were being built, thus laying the foundations of late Victorian Folkestone.

There was a similar need for churches for the rapidly growing local population. In 1862 a small church, St. Peter's, was erected on the Durlocks as a mission to mariners, and it was subsequently enlarged in 1870 and provided with a school for the fishermen's children. Further west another wooden church was opened in 1865; this was St. Michael and All Angels Church, which was given the uncomplimentary name of the 'red barn' on account of its red wooden gables. Later it was replaced by a striking stone church, designed by F. Bodley of Harley Street, in flamboyant Flemish style with a lofty steeple. Its vicar, the Rev. E. Husband was well known for his organ recitals, which attracted large crowds. On the north and west sides of the town, St. John the Baptist's Church was opened in 1879 and St. Saviour's Church in 1885.

There was a corresponding growth in the nonconformist churches. We have already seen something of this in an earlier chapter. The Baptists, who had removed from Mill Bay in 1845, rebuilt their Salem Chapel in Rendezvous Street in 1874. The Congregational Church in Tontine Street was erected in 1856, and a daughter church, the Radnor Park Congregational Church, was built in 1897. The Wesleyan Chapel, built in 1864, at the junction between Grace Hill and Rendezvous Street, became a notable feature of the town with its lofty steeple of 130 feet. The Quakers and the Roman Catholics also had their own buildings in town; and it was said that Folkestone had an excess of churches. But in the Victorian age churches played an important social role in addition to being places of worship. For one thing they were all concerned in the question of education.

SCHOOLS

The story of the Folkestone schools is a long and complicated one, but we propose to state the main facts as briefly as possible. At the beginning of the nineteenth century the only 'free' school was the Harvey Grammar School which still operated in Rendezvous Street. It had very few pupils—only 32 in 1833, and these were taught no more than the three R's. An innovation was made in 1814 when the Headmaster was allowed to take boarders and charge for them. But it did not make much difference to the numbers. The premises of the school were entirely rebuilt in 1845–6, and a new scheme was introduced in 1858 whereby fees were charged for day pupils. The numbers increased to 55 and a new school was needed. This was provided in 1881–2 with a Boarding establishment in Foord Road, and this school continued in use until 1913 when the school moved to new premises in the Cheriton Road.

But in the early years of the nineteenth century the Grammar School had its rivals in two prosperous private schools, one being the Grove House Academy, opened in 1822 and continuing until 1894. The other was an expensive coaching establishment run by the Vicar, the Rev. Thomas Pearce, charging fees of 100 to 150 guineas per annum. These schools were very select and offered a classical, mathematical and commercial education, and opportunities for sea-bathing. There were also a number of private schools for girls and small children. One of these, Fellenburg College in Church Street, ran from 1845 to 1883. It had not less than 100 girls on the roll at any time, and it occupied the site traditionally associated with William Harvey's birth-place. Another school for girls of long-standing was Rockhill House. It began on the Bayle in 1845, and moved to Rockhill House at the corner of Victoria Grove in the 50's. It lasted until 1906. Altogether middle class girls seem to have had better educational opportunities than the boys.

The education of the children of the poor was provided by various religious bodies. As early as 1814 the Folkestone Union Charity School, sponsored by the British and Foreign Bible Society, was opened in the Apollo Room in Queen Square. This ran for some years until in 1835 a new 'British' school was opened. The local M.P., Mr. S. Marjoribanks, bought the former town workhouse in Mill Lane, and offered it to the British Society for a school. In 1856 when Edward Fisher was headmaster there were 451 children on the books; it was run on the 'monitorial system', and there was only one master and one mistress in charge. In 1883 the school was transferred to the new School Board, and in 1887 a new building was erected for 820 children. It was known as the Dover Road Board School.

Another body, the National Society for the Education of the Poor in the Principles of the Established Church, established two 'National' schools, the first in 1852 being connected with the new Christ Church and known as the 'Gun School'; and the second, St. Mary's National School (1855), under the care of the Parish Church. New buildings were erected for these schools which were handsome for their time, and they flourished for over a century. Several of the churches opened schools of their own for their parishioners' children, the Wesleyan school opening in 1871. St. Peter's school followed in 1872 for the benefit of the fishing quarter, and St. Eanswythe's school in 1878 to serve the Bayle area. A Roman Catholic school was provided in 1884, and another National school, All Souls School in Cheriton, in 1887. Many people thought that the town was provided with too many schools, and for years there was considerable resistance to the provision of education for the children of the poor, particularly to the introduction of Board Schools. On one pretext or another the formation of a School Board, which was required by the Education Act of 1870, was put off until 1881, when it became inevitable unless Folkestone could provide within six months accommodation for a further 850 children. There was an angry outcry that this demand was 'thrust upon us: a shilling in the pound rate for the education of other people's children'. However, the law had to be obeyed, and somewhat grudgingly a School Board was elected, and the former British school in Dover Road was adopted, as we have seen, in 1883; but it was not until 1887 that a new building was erected—a delay of seventeen years. This delay was perhaps instrumental in causing the opening of so many church schools between 1871 and 1887, as the Board Schools, like the British schools, gave no religious instruction. Another latent cause for opposition was the reluctance of local parents to send their children to school at all. For many years absenteeism was a constant problem, retarding the educational development of the pupils. Parents were loath to forgo the unpaid labour which their children provided in running errands, delivering goods to hotels, scaring birds, gutting fish and 'minding the baby'. But in spite of difficulties and opposition, by the end of the century the town had a very efficient elementary education service for the local children, according to the educational ideas of the time.

Folkestone's reputation for salubrity and exclusiveness prompted another educational development. Wealthy parents sent their children to private boarding schools which were established in the west end of the town. A host of small exclusive private schools sprang up at the turn of the century, and it was a common sight to see groups of boys or girls walking 'in crocodile' along the Leas, under the supervision of a young teacher. They all wore uniforms of a brilliant colour to distinguish them from commoners and from rival schools. Needless to say, no tradesman's son or daughter was admitted to these schools, however wealthy: east was east and west was west.

PUBLIC TRANSPORT

At the beginning of the twentieth century a new chapter opened with the coming of public transport in the town. Previously private firms hired out wagonettes, flies and cabs to customers, but there was no question of a public service. Oddly enough, there was a service of horse-trams (known locally as 'toast racks') running from Hythe to Seabrook from 1884, and extended to Sandgate in 1891. But Folkestone had nothing like this until 1901 when there was a proposal to run motor-buses from the Town Hall to Shorncliffe Station. (In July, 1901, a small motor wagonette ran from Folkestone to Hythe.) But the first public service vehicle to run was a steam-driven wagonette called the 'Pioneer', which began operations in 1902. It seated twenty-two persons, had a vertical boiler and a canvas curtain to protect the passengers from smuts. It was driven off the road by the competition from the Folkestone Motors Company Ltd., which started up in 1903. This Company ran a number of large patent coaches with huge wheels 5 feet in diameter; they were painted a bright yellow, and were familiarly known as the

'Yellow Pots'. Other coaches known as 'Pullman Cars' were added to the service and they were a common sight in the early days. There were other rival coach operators, and sometimes as many as six coaches would be waiting outside the Town Hall for customers. They would not move off until a reasonable number of passengers were aboard, and then there was often a race between the coaches along the Cheriton Road to Shorn-cliffe, to the amusement of local spectators. But it was Messrs. A. V. Wills's yellow buses which supplied the first reliable service, and his company dominated the scene until the East Kent Road Car Company was formed in 1916. There was a proposal in the early days to start a service of electric trams in Folkestone, but a poll of the town taken in 1905 showed opposition to the erection of overhead power wires, and with the growing success of the motor buses, the scheme was dropped.

THE INFIRMARY

In the middle of the century steps were taken to cater for the needs of the sick. In 1845, Dr. Donnelly, a retired Naval Surgeon, founded a Dispensary, maintained by voluntary subscriptions, to give free medical advice and medicine to the poor. The first premises were next to the original Grammar School in Rendezvous Street. In 1864, owing to the increase in demand, a lease was taken of a house, number 20 Dover Road (subsequently occupied by Messrs. Pickford), and three beds for casualties were maintained. In 1886 sixty-eight patients were admitted, and there were 2,093 out-patients. Further expansion was necessary, and the forthcoming Jubilee of Queen Victoria was taken as a suitable occasion to establish a modern hospital. In 1887, Lord Radnor offered an acre of land adjacent to Radnor Park, and the Victoria Hospital was built in 1889 and opened on 3rd July, 1890, by the contemporary Duke of Edinburgh. This hospital has been of immense value to the people of Folkestone.

It will be realized that with the great expansion of the town the work of the Council increased enormously. The various Local Government Acts extended the powers of the local Council, and this in turn necessitated a growth in the permanent administrative staff. During the century the town was well served by its Council members and by its officers, who for years had to work in inadequate premises. And although the significance of the town as a limb of the Cinque Ports has dwindled with the passage of time, the Corporation still carries on its historic traditions.

CHAPTER ELEVEN

THE FIRST WORLD WAR:
THE RECOVERY

THE summer season of 1914 was in full swing when the German war broke out. Folkestone was crowded with visitors enjoying a hot summer, listening to the bands and bathing in the sea. There was a mood of confidence at first—it would all be over in three months, they said. But soon various changes were noticed. Men began to appear in uniform on the Leas, especially officers; there was a great exodus of German and Austrian waiters from the hotels; the visitors began to melt away. Folkestone was a little too close to the continent to be comfortable, and there was always the risk of bombardment from enemy cruisers. So the hotels emptied and the season came to an early end.

It is not intended to give a detailed account of the events of the war in Folkestone, but rather to indicate some of the changes it brought about. The seriousness of the conflict came vividly home to the town when in the third week of August boat-loads of Belgian refugees, exhausted, destitute and hungry, came into the harbour. Day after day, week after week, they came in fishing boats and colliers, and meals, clothes and beds had to be found at short notice. In the first months of the war 64,500 refugees came to the town for succour, and it is to the credit of the townsfolk and the Belgian Committee for Refugees that so much was done at short notice. Many were sent to new centres inland, but it is estimated that at one period as many as fifteen to twenty thousand refugees had to be accommodated in the town. Among the refugees were Belgian soldiers, some wounded, who had been cut off from their divisions in the onslaught of the German advance into Belgium. The war was very real.

The next change was the arrival of thousands of young recruits in training on Shorncliffe Camp. As the war progressed the number of soldiers increased and Folkestone became an armed camp. They were soon joined by Canadian forces, and eventually by the Americans. The streets of the town thronged with men in military uniforms of different kinds. From March, 1915 onwards, Folkestone became the chief base for the transport of troops to France; and during the whole period of the war seven million men were ferried across to the battlefields of France without loss. Every day columns of soldiers would march in full kit down the slope road to the harbour, singing the nostalgic songs of the war years and joking as they went along. It was heartbreaking to think that many would never return.

To accommodate them while they waited for the cross-channel boat, or stayed over night for the crossing, whole blocks of hotels, boarding houses and private dwellings were commandeered by the military, and the occupants forced to find other places to live. All the houses in Marine Parade, Marine Terrace and Lower Sandgate Road were taken as temporary shelters for the men. And as boat-loads of wounded were brought back to the port, they were taken to nursing homes and large hotels which were converted into temporary hospitals. Later still it was a common sight to see wounded men in blue hospital uniforms hobbling on crutches as they took the air and sun during their convalescence. The townspeople went to great trouble to provide comforts, refreshments and entertainment for soldiers billeted in the town or in training on the camp.

During these years one was very much aware of the war in Folkestone, and one felt one was very near the firing line as the noise of the guns thundered across the Channel. Actually the town did not suffer greatly from enemy action, which, for the most part, was foiled by the defence. It had no bombardments from the sea, thanks to the Dover Patrol, and only once or twice was there serious attack from the air. The worst damage occurred on 25th May, 1917, when a flight of 17 Gotha aeroplanes returning from a raid on London, shed their remaining load of bombs on the town as they made for home. The damage and loss of life would have been slight but for the devastation wrought by a single bomb which fell in the middle of Tontine Street at a busy shopping hour. The carnage was horrible, 71 civilians being killed and 94 injured in this street alone. This was the first daylight air-raid, and it took everyone by surprise;

but although Zeppelin raids and moonlight air raids were a constant menace from then on, no serious damage was done to the town. More serious was the anxiety and fear aroused by the long sleepless nights of watching; and whenever enemy planes were heard approaching, the anti-aircraft guns would roar out and searchlights probe the sky. A further effect was the total black-out imposed on the town, and pedestrians were obliged to grope their way along the darkened streets at night.

The submarine menace was an ever-present concern, and watchers from the cliffs would see 'incidents' out at sea, and from time to time exploding depth charges would cause a rumbling tremor as of an earthquake. To assist in countering the submarine attacks an airship station was established on the cliffs at Capel, and small dirigible airships could often be seen patrolling the shore off the town, or returning at a low altitude over the houses. The huge air hangars at Capel were on one occasion the target of six raiding enemy destroyers, but they missed their mark and did no damage; but on their return journey they were intercepted by H.M.S. 'Brooke' and 'Swift' which sank two of their number. Another target was the camp of the Zulu and Chinese Labour Corps, situated at the foot of Caesar's Camp, but they were never hit.

Altogether Folkestone suffered little from direct enemy action, but the town grew dilapidated and dirty, and the roads, being subject to an enormous amount of military traffic, which they could not bear, degenerated into mud tracks. Gone were the days of bands, concert parties, and fashionable holidaymakers: instead, the place looked sad and exhausted with the constant wear and tear of the war effort.

When the peace came the adjustment to the new conditions was slow and painful. The bitter experiences of the war changed the climate of men's thoughts, and a return to the heyday of Edwardian fashion and manners was unthinkable. For one thing, money was scarce and prices were high; for another, work for the returning forces was hard to find and unemployment was rife. Slowly the boarding houses, hotels and private dwellings were derequisitioned and furbished up. The hotels on the Leas were painted and opened for the holiday maker, but things were not easy. It was not possible to recruit labour on the old terms, with domestic staff living in and working for a pittance. Men returning from the war had another attitude to their work—they were more independent and less inclined to servility; many emigrated to the colonies and to America.

Then again, the wealthy families who came before the war found fresh fields for their holidays. It became fashionable to take advantage of the improved railway and boat services to go to the Riviera. The value of the French franc had dropped to a low level and it was much cheaper (and more exciting) to go abroad—to Nice, Monte Carlo and a dozen Mediterranean resorts. So the large and exclusive hotels which used to cater for the upper classes found themselves in a new and uncomfortable situation. Their former clientele had dwindled, and the same problem affected other parts of the town. It was a different world that emerged in 1919.

In order to thrive as a seaside resort it was necessary for Folkestone to adapt itself to the new circumstances. If it could not attract the clientele of the pre-war years, it must find a new one. And this is what it did. Fortunately we had on the Town Council a body of enterprising and devoted Councillors who made it their policy to restore the Town's prosperity by appealing to the middle classes who brought their young families down to the seaside for the annual fortnight's holiday. The west end grew less exclusive and expensive and appealed to the upper middle classes; the lower part of the town welcomed the eastender and the trippers who began to arrive by bus.

Another urgent task was the provision of housing for men returning from the forces. There was a great shortage of houses, and the town had hitherto made little provision for the working classes. Under the Housing Act of 1890 the town had built only forty-three houses; but between 1919 and 1938 a total of 767 houses were provided on a large housing estate on the north-east side of the town, more than half (461) of them being three-bedroom houses. The main thoroughfare of the estate was named Wood Avenue, after R. G. Wood, an enterprising Mayor of the time. The town also extended its boundaries, absorbing Cheriton and Sandgate in 1934. This growth necessitated further extension of all the town services. For instance, the Council was aware of the need for further development of the drainage system; several new sewers were installed and the effluent was discharged much further out to sea beyond Copt Point, thus freeing the east sands of the taint of sewage. This development enabled the east foreshore to be used for sea bathing.

While these and other tasks were being carried out in the town, several other schemes were undertaken in the development of the seaside resort. One of the first was the laying out of the foreshore alongside the Marine Gardens with a permanent amusement centre built by Lord Radnor. This contained roundabouts, dodgems, a motor-boating lake, a skating rink, and a Rotunda containing slot-machines. An open-air swimming bath was also provided, which became the centre for cross-channel swimming training. The Marina was established by the Manor Office and the various amusements were let out to individual enterprise. Adjacent to it the Council built the Marine Pavilion (1926), as a centre for variety shows, dancing and skating. In 1927 followed the Leas Cliff Hall, which replaced the old Leas Shelter. In the same year the Council took over the functions of the former Folkestone Amusements Association, providing bands for the bandstands and music in the new Leas Cliff Hall. At this period several seaside resorts competed in the provision of symphony orchestras; Folkestone ran a small permanent orchestra for several years, and visiting orchestras also played there. The Hall was also used for dancing, variety and for public meetings.

In 1924 Lord Radnor gave the East Cliff area and the Warren for the enjoyment of the town. This gift extended the amenities of the resort considerably, and the East Cliff area began to be developed. The East Cliff Pavilion was built to provide refreshment for visitors and new lawns were laid. With the improvement of the east sands by the removal of rocks, the opportunity was taken of landscaping the cliff with terraced walks and flower beds, and a rock garden and path were made down Baker's Gap to the seashore. In 1935 a new raised promenade was constructed and called 'Coronation Parade', which provided a new walk for visitors and a protection for the unstable cliffs. The Warren had always been an attraction to ramblers and naturalists. The Council now provided facilities for camping, and a bathing station was built there for the convenience of bathers.

On the West Cliff a new departure was a zigzag path, built in 1921, and landscaped and planted with flowers, and leading

THE FIRST WORLD WAR: THE RECOVERY

down to the Lower Sandgate Road. This was a much appreciated feature as it gave easy access to the seaside even for
invalids in bath-chairs. Another departure was to increase the
amount of floral display in as many public places as possible.
Folkestone adopted the title of 'Floral Folkestone' and the
general appearance of the town was enhanced. In 1928 a new
flower garden of some six acres was created near the Central
Station in a former clay-pit from which brick earth had been
extracted. This became the Kingsnorth Gardens, where a
constant display of flowers is maintained. In Radnor Park old
shrubberies and unwanted fences were done away with, thus
increasing the sense of spaciousness. The sportsman was not
overlooked; an excellent sports ground already existed on the
Cheriton Road. This was enlarged and further facilities
provided. Tennis and bowls were available in the Radnor
Park, and golf on the 18-hole golf course under the hills, and
on a miniature course at Copt Point.

A still more remarkable attraction was provided in the
summer of 1924. Owing to the collapse of a portion of the
cliffs at East Wear Bay, the site of a Roman Villa was revealed.
We have already referred to this in Chapter Two; and when
facilities were provided for people to visit the site hundreds of
visitors wandered round the foundations re-creating in their
minds the kind of life the Roman inhabitants formerly lived
there. The site stimulated a keen interest in local history, and
but for the coming of the Second World War, would have been
a permanent asset to the town as the Romano-British palace at
Fishbourne has proved to be to Chichester. But the difficulties
produced by the next world war caused the Council to have
the site filled in; and much of it still remains under the turf
beside the Wear Bay Road.

All these interests and facilities, as well as those of the pre-war
period still in existence, proved very attractive to the new type
of visitors, and during the thirties the town reached a new level
of popularity and prosperity.

CHAPTER TWELVE

THE SECOND WORLD WAR: FOLKESTONE TODAY

ONLY a few hours after war was declared in September, 1939, the Air Raid sirens sounded, and everyone thought that the last war had begun again. But they were mistaken. This war was to be infinitely more devastating than the last, and some of the crucial battles were to be fought right overhead. At first Folkestone was rated as a safe area and thousands of children from other districts were sent here for 'safety'. It was not long before they had to be sent back to safer places. In May, 1940, the French ports in the Straits of Dover fell to the advancing enemy, who now were at our very doors. The British Army had to be rescued from the beaches of Dunkirk, and destroyers and all sorts of boats brought the exhausted troops into the harbour, and they were sent to assembly points inland. In September came the Battle of Britain in which fighter aircraft from Hawkinge set off to do battle against superior numbers over the whole of the south-east region. Some of the enemy planes were shot down and fell in the town itself.

Not surprisingly there was a great exodus; in a few weeks 35,000 residents left the town, which became a prohibited area. With the threat of invasion looming up the military set up a system of concrete blocks which bisected the town. They ran from the top of Castle Hill Avenue, across Radnor Park to the foot of the Downs. All the beaches were festooned with barbed wire, some sections were mined, and iron scaffolding placed along the shore. Gun batteries were placed on the Leas and on East Cliff, and all roads into the town had their tank traps and fortified blockhouses. The very hills were scarred with the long chalk trench line of a tank-trap.

The town was under constant attack from the air and extensive damage was caused by bombs, parachute mines, shells from across the Channel, flying bombs and machine gunning. The long story of the town's agony cannot be told here; but it should be read by those who come here for the first time, so that they may understand the enormous problems of rehabilitation which faced the Council at the end of it all. According to the official report 663 projectiles fell upon the town, causing 901 casualties, of which 123 were fatal. Some 600 flying bombs were shot down off the beaches (so saving many lives), and about 500 shells fell in the harbour. Some 550 dwellings were destroyed and over 10,000 other properties were extensively damaged. The part of the town which suffered most damage was to the east of Tontine Street up as far as Canterbury Road. The area immediately behind the harbour was almost completely devastated. The only parts of old Folkestone that remained relatively intact were the High Street, the Bayle and the Parish Church. Folkestone was called by a distinguished visitor 'the abomination of desolation'. Yet most of the town's public buildings survived, the only major casualty being Christ Church in Sandgate Road, which was demolished except for the tower. Another loss was the Roman Villa site which had received considerable damage; after the war the Council decided to preserve what was left by filling the area in and turfing it.

The problems before the Council when peace returned may well be imagined. The town had lost its income from rates and from its main industry—the holiday catering industry. The native residents began to return to their homes, which needed repair or replacement. The shops were empty and most of them had no glass fronts, being boarded up or shuttered with black canvas frames. The hotels could not function until they had been renovated after military occupation. Not least, the work of removing the defences had to be accomplished before anything else could function. All the concrete blocks had to be removed, the gun sites dismantled, and the beaches cleared of mines, tank-traps, barbed wire and iron scaffolding. It is to the great credit of all concerned that so much was accomplished in so short a time. To quote the official account published by the Town Council: 'Folkestone was among the first of the fortified resorts to clear its defence works, and as a result of this and the energy displayed by all concerned with the resumption of the business life of the town, by the 1946 season, it proved possible to bring into commission a little over half the hotels and boarding houses, and during 1947 to receive a number of Conferences.'

During the next twenty years the town gradually regained its status as one of the most attractive seaside resorts on the south coast. The scars of war were healed, the devastated areas by the harbour were replanned and rebuilt and the visitors returned. The policy of employing extensive floral displays was renewed and the town eventually recovered its beauty and neatness. There were two losses after the war; one was the destruction of the Victoria Pier by fire in 1945, and the closing of the Pleasure Gardens Theatre in 1960. One development has been the building of a new Civic Centre in Castle Hill Avenue, where all the municipal business is carried out.

At the moment, extensive alterations are taking place in the centre of the town to accommodate motor traffic; old landmarks are disappearing and new buildings are going up. There is a feeling of change in the air; even in the sphere of government the ancient Borough is to be amalgamated with other local bodies, and its old independence will be sacrificed. We hope that this short account will serve as a record of the Borough's long and honourable history.

Since 1973 many changes have taken place. As in other towns there has been a certain amount of demolition and rebuilding, partly owing to the need for a through traffic route, and partly in anticipation of a channel tunnel. A number of Victorian hotels have been demolished, several rows of dwelling houses lost, and some of the sites left derelict; and where replacements have been made, the architecture has not improved the townscape. In spite of these changes Folkestone still retains much of its charm.

A FOLKESTONE CHRONOLOGY

B.C.

There are indications of the presence of Neolithic man, Bronze Age man and Iron Age man, especially at the foot of the hills to the north of the town. There is evidence also of Belgic occupation, particularly in the British villa found on East Cliff.

A.D.

80–350   Roman settlement. Several villas on East Cliff.

100   First century cemetery at Cheriton.

600   Saxon burial ground on Dover Hill.

630   King Eadbald built a church dedicated to St. Peter and St. Paul for his daughter Eanswythe, where she became the founder Abbess of the first nunnery in England. Eadbald also built a castle or fort on the Bayle.

640   Nunnery and church attacked by the Danes. Death of St. Eanswythe.

927   Church and nunnery restored by King Athelstan.

1052   Godwyn, Earl of Kent pillaged the town and destroyed the church.

1086   Domesday Book. Folkestone valued at £100.

1095   New Priory founded on the site of the old Nunnery by Nigel de Muneville.

1138   The cliff on which the Priory was built considered unsafe. New Priory and church built, outside the castle, by Wm. D'Averanches and dedicated to St. Mary and St. Eanswythe. This was the foundation of the present church. Destroyed in 1216. Rebuilt about 1220, the date of the present chancel.

1138   Relics of St. Eanswythe carried in solemn procession from the old Priory to the new church.

1205   Jeffrey Fitz-Peter procures a market to be held weekly on Thursday. Since this date Folkestone has been a market town and it had two fairs a year. A cattle fair in Cow Street (Sandgate Road), and a Toy Fair on the Bayle.

1215   Wm. d'Albrinces obtains confirmation of 1205 market.

1216   King John and his court at Folkestone.

1236   Extension of Parish Church.

1263   Lords of the Manor had a capital messuage, with a garden, courtyard, dovecote, three mills, 400 acres of well-stocked park, 50 acres of wood and three fish ponds. They also owned a profitable quarry here.

1299   Folkestone (Simon Adam, Master) provides one 'coga' or cock-boat and 24 companions, for Royal Service.

1313   Charter of Incorporation constituting the 'Mayor, Jurats, and Commonalty'. Confirmed and enlarged in 1326.

1349   Sir John de Segrave secures renewal of 1215 market with the addition of another weekly market on Tuesdays.

1378   Combined forces of French and Scots despoiled the town.

1390   Sir John de Clinton obtains a grant for a market to be held on Wednesdays and a yearly fair on the Vigil and Day of St. Giles.

1467   Masters of The Boat of Folkestone seized a Spanish vessel with wine and contents worth £533.

1472   Vineyards noted in the town.

1522   French attack local fishermen.

1535   Priory surrendered. When pulled down, the stone was used for Sandgate Castle.

1539   Sandgate Castle built by Henry VIII.

1542   Earl of Hertford's Minstrels performed at Master Baker's.

1543   Henry VIII visits the town to consider the harbour.

1545   Enlargement of Corporation; 24 common Councillors added.

1555   Mayor's salary £2/13/4. Town Clerk's £4. Town Drummer's 33/4.

1564   The Queen's 'bereward' visits the town.

1565   Folkestone contains 120 inhabited houses; twenty-five fishing boats.
        The Queen's Players visit the town.
        Mr. Rolf comes 'to see the place of an harbour here'.

1573   Queen Elizabeth visited Folkestone.

1578   Wm. Harvey born in Folkestone.

1580   One-hundred men at work in Folkestone quarries for Dover Haven.

1584   Sir Richard Greynvile proposes construction of a haven (not carried out).

1588   Spanish Armada. Preparations to resist invasion.

1600   Queen's Players in Folkestone.

1605   Joan Harvey buried in Parish Church.
        Poorhouse noted on corner of Grace Hill.

1624   Plague in town.

1627	Folkestone received two pieces of ordnance for defence against the French.
1628	Dr. Harvey published *De Motu Cordis*.
1636	Dr. Wm. Harvey secured from the Crown lease of part of Prior's Leas for town use.
1639	A cess granted to raise £10 to fit out a ship of war.
1651	Publication of Harvey's *De Generatione Animalium*.
1657	Death of Dr. Harvey.
1665	Outbreak of plague.
1674	Harvey Grammar School founded by Sir Eliab Harvey, from bequest left by Dr. Wm. Harvey; school sited in Rendezvous Street; transferred to new buildings in Foord Road in 1882; removed again to Cheriton Road in 1913.
1697	Manor of Folkestone alienated to Jacob Desbouverie.
1698	Baptists established in Folkestone by Thomas Carr. In 1729 they built a meeting house in Mill Bay, where they continued until 1845 when they erected Salem Chapel in Rendezvous Street. Rebuilt 1874.
1699	Inhabitants called upon to restore harbour.
1705	Collapse of part of nave of Parish Church in a storm.
1720	Small-pox epidemic—145 victims.
1752	Act for widening road from Dover to Barham Downs. Enlarged through Folkestone and Hythe.
1765	Small-pox epidemic—158 victims.
1766	Act for support and preservation of Parish Church and lower part of town from ravages of the sea.
1773	Mr. Wilson, ship-builder, established boat-building in Sandgate.
1774	Bayle Theatre opened.
1784	Extensive landslide of West Cliff. Debris used later to form Lower Sandgate Road walks and gardens.
1787	'Two elegant bathing machines for the recreation of gentlemen and ladies.'
1790	Society of Friends' new Meeting House built in Dover Street.
1794	Land for Shorncliffe Camp acquired for War Office.
1795	Advertisement in *Kentish Gazette*, 24th June, 'sea bathing at Folkestone ... bathing machines will be regularly attended every day during the season'.
1796	Act for paving, repairing and cleansing the town.
1802	Wreck of Dutch East Indiaman, the 'Vryheid', at Dymchurch.

1805–6   Martello Towers erected for defence of the coast.

1807   Act of Parliament for constructing a Pier and Harbour. Folkestone Harbour Company formed.

1808   Foundation stone of Harbour Pier laid.

1811   Silver tokens issued by John Boxer.

1814   Folkestone Union Charity School—British and Foreign Schools' Society—founded in the 'Appollo Room'. In 1835 the school moved to the former Folkestone Workhouse, then on the site of Dover Road School. The present Dover Road School on the same site was opened in 1887. Re-named 'Hillside' in 1951. New Hillside Secondary School for Boys opened at Park Farm in 1958.

1824   Wesleyans meet at Elgar's Yard.

1825   Act of Parliament enabling Lord Radnor to grant leases for building on Folkestone estate.

1828   Lord Radnor constructs Lower Sandgate Road.

1829   Police Force appointed. First two constables Matthew Pearson and William Downing.

1830   Cistern House adopted as Town Hall. Built by Lord Radnor and hired to Corporation. Demolished 1858.

1835   British School opened in the former workhouse in Dover Road. The Board School opened on same site in 1887. Municipal Reform Act. Town has a new constitution.

1840   Original Guildhall, at corner of Church Street and Rendezvous Street demolished. It had occupied the site since the mid-sixteenth century at least.

1842   First Gas Works established on the beach, west of the future Pavilion Hotel. First supply to inhabitants 29th December. Private consumers 60; street lamps 30.

1843   South Eastern Railway Co. bought up Harbour for £18,000. Railway line from London opened: the first temporary station being somewhere in the fields between Guildhall Street and Cheriton Road, just west of the viaduct. The viaduct was completed in December, and the first permanent station (the Junction), opened 18th December, 1843. Meanwhile, the Harbour had been cleared of shingle and mud, and the first cross-channel Packet operated from 1st August. First boat was the 'William Wallace'. Harbour House with Clock Tower built, and Pavilion Hotel started. (Hotel enlarged in 1845 and 1850.)

1846   'The Dispensary' founded in Rendezvous Street. Transferred to Dover Road (Pickford's Site) in 1863 with 3 beds.

In 1864 named the 'Folkestone Dispensary and Infirmary'.
(Royal Victoria Hospital opened in 1890.)
Lower Sandgate Road re-constructed.

1848 Building of Guildhall Street begun. (Originally Shellons
Lane.)
Plans for building Tontine Street.
Act for supplying the Parish and Township with water.
Whale taken off Folkestone.

1849 Branch line to Harbour, swing bridge and Terminal
Station built.

1850 Christ Church built.

1851 Rev. Matthew Woodward became Vicar of Folkestone.

1852 Opening of the 'New National School' in Cheriton Road
(Gun School). Christ Church School. New Christ Church
Primary School opened in Brockman Road in 1955.
Wesleyan Chapel built in Sandgate Road.

1854 St. Mary's National School built; opened 1855.

1855 An Act to extend the limits of the Borough of Folkestone,
to enable the Corporation to construct a Market House,
make new streets and improvements, and to pave, light,
drain and otherwise improve the said Borough.
Queen Victoria visited Shorncliffe Camp.
Charles Dickens stayed for 3 months at 3 Albion Villas.

1856 Congregational Church built in Tontine Street.

1857 Cheriton Road Cemetery opened.

1858 First Post Office Pillar Box erected.

1859 Restoration of Parish Church begun.

1860 Marine Terrace commenced building.

1861 Present Town Hall opened. 'Promenade' Pier begun.

1862 Bouverie Square commenced.
St. Peter's Church built. (Later enlarged, 1870.)

1863 Holmesdale Terrace commenced. New houses built on the
Leas (Royal Terrace).

1864 Extensive landslips in the Warren.
Grant of sites of St. Michael's and Holy Trinity Churches.

1865 Clifton Gardens, East, built.
St. Michael's Church opened; first building of wood.
Wesleyan Chapel, Grace Hill erected.

1866 Old Gas Works on beach demolished. Works removed to
Foord Road.

1867 Promenade Bands organized.

1868 Natural History Society founded.
Holy Trinity Church opened.

1869   Bathing Establishment (Marina) opened.
        Restoration of chancel of Parish Church.

1870   Natural History Society opened Museum in the old
        Sessions House in High Street (formerly Wesleyan Metho-
        dist Church).

1871   Wesleyan School opened under Chapel (closed 1926).

1872   St. Peter's School opened.

1874   Opening of Hythe and Sandgate Railway.
        Radnor Club opened.

1877   Clifton Gardens, West built.
        Sandgate Toll Gate abolished.

1878   Bradstone Hall built.
        Wreck of 'Grosser Kurfurst' off Sandgate.

1879   Public Library opened on the Bayle.

1880   First shaft of proposed Channel Tunnel driven.

1881   Shorncliffe Station opened.
        Harvey Statue unveiled.

1884   Central Station built. First named 'Cheriton Arch'; re-
        named 'Radnor Park' in 1886, and finally re-named
        'Central Station' in 1895.
        St. Andrew's Convalescent Home opened.

1885   Leas Lift opened, 16th September.
        Mundella School opened—originally the North Board
        School and later the North Council School.
        Queen's Hotel built.

1886   Art Treasures Exhibition opened.
        Radnor Park opened.

1888   Victoria Pier opened July. Switchback Railway built.
        Pleasure Gardens Theatre opened, with Pleasure Gardens.
        New Library and Museum on Grace Hill opened by
        Sir E. Watkin.

1889   Elham Valley Line to Canterbury opened.
        St. John the Baptist's Church opened at Foord.

1891   Hythe and Sandgate Horse Trams began. Operated until
        1921.
        Wreck of 'Benvenue' off Sandgate.

1893   Folkestone Amusements Association formed.
        Lower Sandgate Road Gardens laid out.
        Marine Gardens Bandstand built.
        Sandgate Hill lift opened. Closed 1918.

1894   Leas Shelter opened.

1895   Lower Leas Bandstand erected.

1896   Technical School opened.

1897   Sydney Street School opened.
       Radnor Park Congregational Church opened.
1898   Electricity Works started.
       Folkestone Race Course opened.
1901   First Motor Omnibus Service started between Folkestone and Hythe.
1902   Leas Pavilion opened as a 'superior' Tea Room with music.
       West Leas Bandstand rebuilt; transferred from Metropole Hotel Gardens.
       Hill Road constructed below Downs by Lord Radnor.
1903   Grand Hotel built. Opened 1905.
1904   West Leas Lift (Metropole) opened 31st March. Closed 1939.
       Grand Hotel built. Opened 1905.
1905   Cricket Ground opened (Cheriton Road).
       Folkestone County School for Girls founded. Eight pupils met in Masonic Hall, Grace Hill. Moved to Pelham House, 1906, then to Penfold House, Coolinge Lane, 1921.
1909   Morehall School opened.
1910   Electric Theatre (Savoy) opened. Building was first planned as a theatre, and partly built in 1902. Later it was a garage, then a skating rink, next a cinema, finally a Bingo Hall.
       First part of Marine Promenade built.
1912   Queen's Cinema, Tontine Street opened.
       Playhouse Cinema opened.
       Central Cinema opened.
1913   Leas and West Cliff Walks leased to Folkestone Corporation.
1914   First World War. Voluntary organizations entertain troops.
1915   Belgian refugees crowd into the town.
       Harbour became chief port for despatch of troops and goods to France.
1917   Air Raid on town on 25th May, caused heavy casualties. 71 killed and 96 injured.
1922   Zigzag Path constructed on Leas.
1924   Roman Villas excavated on East Cliff.
1925   Hawkinge Cemetery opened.
1926   Marine Gardens Pavilion completed.
1927   Leas Cliff Hall opened by Prince Henry.
1928   Kingsnorth Gardens opened on site of clay pit.
1929   Arthur Brough's first season at Leas Pavilion. After being used as a Tea Room, with Billiards and 'Drawing-Room

Entertainments', a stage was built, and Concert Party Seasons were started. The first Repertory Company under the direction of Grant Anderson came in 1928, followed by the Brough Players in October, 1929.

1931   Bobby's Store transferred from Rendezvous Street to new premises on site of old Albion Terrace.

1934   Cheriton and Sandgate incorporated in Borough of Folkestone.
East Cliff Pavilion opened.

1935   Astoria Cinema built on site of Maestrani's Restaurant. Later renamed 'Odeon' Cinema.
Following a landslip, houses in Fishmarket demolished and rebuilt.

1936   Open-air Swimming Pool on beach opened.

1937   New Labour Exchange opened in Ingles Lane (formerly in Tontine Street). Transferred to old GPO in Sandgate Road in 1957.

1938   Cheriton Branch Library and Clinic opened.

1939   Harcourt School opened.
World War II evacuees from London arrived 1940; Folkestone schoolchildren evacuated to Wales. Resident population reduced to 12,000.

1940   Isolation Hospital destroyed by bomb (b. 1897).

1942   Civic Restaurant opened at Woodward Hall. Closed May, 1946.

1945   Victoria Pier destroyed by fire on Whit Monday.

1953   New sea wall completed at Sandgate.

1955   New Bus Station opened in Bouverie Square.

1956   Hawkinge Crematorium opened.

1958   Marina (Folkestone Bathing Establishment) closed.
Visit of Queen and Prince Philip.

1959   Metropole Hotel closed; New Metropole Arts Centre and Restaurant opened 1961.

1960   Sunny Sands Restaurant opened. East Cliff Sands developed.
Wood Avenue Branch Library opened.
Pleasure Gardens Theatre closed.

1961   Hawkinge Aerodrome closed.

1962   Central Station rebuilt and line electrified.
Majestic Hotel (West Cliff) closed.
Queen's Hotel closed.

1967   New Civic Centre opened.

1970   Trinity Pilot Station erected.

1972	Car Ferry Terminal opened at Harbour.

1972   Car Ferry Terminal opened at Harbour.
Welfare Insurance Building opened on the Leas.
Northern Distributor Road under construction 1972–5.

1973   Victory Insurance Building erected on site of Majestic Hotel.

1974   Shepway District Council takes over from Folkestone Borough Council.
First part of Pavilion Hotel demolished. Burstin Motel begun. Lyndhurst Hotel demolished.
Tontine Street Congregational Church demolished.

1975   Pedestrian Precinct formed in Sandgate Road.
Wampach Hotel demolished.

1976   Multistorey Car Park opened.
Demolition of Wesleyan Church on Grace Hill.
Bouverie House built.
New Wesleyan Church opened in Sandgate Road.

1978   New Magistrate's Court built. (Opened 1979).

1980   Demolition of houses in Foord Road area.
Remainder of Pavilion Hotel demolished.

A NOTE ON PLACE-NAMES

WE HAVE REFERRED to the importance of place-names in giving us clues to the origins of settlements. The Place-Name Society has worked for years on Kentish names but no results have yet been published, and we are obliged to explore for ourselves. Wallenberg's volumes, important as they are, make little allowance for possible pre-Saxon origins. He says: 'Apart from the names of a small number of rivers, the names of Keltic origin may almost be counted on the five fingers of the hand.' Ekwall's *Dictionary of English Place-Names* refers only tentatively to British forms, yet many names can only be explained with reference to pre-Saxon elements.

We should be prepared to admit that immigrant peoples would adopt names of places and geographical features from the natives living on the spot; and that they would add their own forms and so producing hybrids which have come down to us, often in attenuated forms. A name like 'Bredon' is such an example. The 'bre' and 'don' elements are Celtic, and signify 'headland' and 'hill' respectively. In Leicestershire the Saxons took the name and added 'on the hill' thus producing a tautological form, 'Bredon-on-the-Hill'. In Kent they added 'stone', thus producing 'Bredenstone', the name they gave to the western Pharos at Dover. Similarly Dover is another Celtic name from 'dwr' (water) and 'bre' (headland); hence the Latin form of 'Dubris'—'the stream by the hill'. Many Kentish names can be traced back in this way, such as Romney, Winchelsea, Goodwin Sands, Chatham, etc. We have attempted to account for the name of Folkestone on the same principle.

Note on p. 44. According to the Customals criminals condemned to death should 'fall in the valley of Stodway'. Nobody now knows for certain where that was, but we may get a hint from the entry in Matilda Averanch's inventory (see p. 31) which includes certain fields at 'Stodwey-super-le-Dune'. The Stodway was probably the 'steed-way' or horse track on the top of the Downs. It was probably the Crete Road, from which criminals were hurled down the steep precipitous slope above the present Wingate chalk-pit, or even the valley of Holy Well. A victim, bound and blindfolded, would hardly survive such a fall. At Dover they threw the victims over Sharpness (? Shakespeare Cliff).

Another local mystery concerns the 'Tiddiman's Steps' up the eastern edge of Sugar Loaf Hill and on to Crete Road. The name may be a corrupt form of 'Deadman's Steps'—being the route taken by the victim and his executioners to the top of the Downs. 'Deadman' was perhaps assimilated to 'Tiddiman' by folk stymology, since it was a common local name. But this is only a guess.

A JEU D'ESPRIT

FROM A NEWSPAPER cutting dated February, 1853, advocating the Voluntary System in the matter of Church Rates at Folkestone.

On the south-eastern coast stands an old boro' town,
That has lately been rising to fame and renown;
As the sea flows below, and high hills stand behind,
Surpassing in beauty most spots of the kind,
It deserves to be known by the seekers of health,
Who leave London yearly, expending their wealth.
The original streets on two slopes are so narrow,
That a fly cannot easily pass a wheelbarrow:
In crooks, corners and alleys, these old streets abound,
Where a stranger bewildered may sometimes be found.
Tradition asserts that the gap in the rock,
Where the houses are built, was produced by a shock
Of an earthquake—and then, as the moon gave her light,
The erections were made in the silence of night.
This remark may be laugh'd at by men not a few,
Although others on searching may find it is true.

The Town has its Aldermen, Council and Mayor,
Council-Chamber, Policemen—an annual fair—
A Town Hall and Recorder—a mineral spring,
With a modern made ruin, a capital thing!
Since the Railway thro' tunnels, and viaducts over
Deep vallies, was finished from London to Dover,
New houses have rapidly sprung and appeared—
Brick by brick, board by board, they are honestly reared—
And Visitors flock to the Pier and the Lees,
To enhale what is deemed a salubrious breeze.

In the spring a new source of amusement was planned,
And a meeting convened to engage a fine Band,
This meeting, harmonious, straight-forward fair,
Elected as Chairman, His Worship the Mayor,
And passed four Resolutions the plan to effect,
Against which not a Sinner was found to object.

A Subscription was opened, and names were put down
With certain amounts for the good of the Town:
To please and be pleas'd was the rule of the day,
And the meeting broke up in the usual way.
So a band was engag'd—ten youths 'cross the water
Came o'er to enliven each mother and daughter:
Three Clarionets, Ophieclide, French-horns and Flute
With notes sweet and soothing, surpassing the Lute;
A Trombone and two Cornets—all finely in tune,
Were play'd through the summer, commencing in June.
We had overtures, polkas, slow pieces, quadrilles,
Chords in full, and staccato—abundance of trills—
And by those who no difference in music can tell,
The performance was thought to pass off very well.

To men of reflection sad thoughts will arise,
As o'er the subscription list wandered their eyes,
When they see who subscribe, and add up the amount
The Treasurer received on the credit account.
Take the number of names, say, one hundred and fifty,
Embracing all grades from the rich to the thrifty—
And out of that number one hundred at least
Are men, who, in Vestry, support Church and Priest.
Above two hundred pounds on the papers appear,
Freely given the Visitors' spirits to cheer;
Of which, full three-fourths came from those who profess
To be ready to rescue their Church in distress.
Thus with ease for amusement the funds can be found;
Better far than by taxing the Parish all round;
But when old mother Church *asks her sons*, for a gift
Very few can be found who will lend her a lift:
Then, the Vestry must meet, and the parish must pay,
Or the worship and building decline and decay.

.   .   .   .

Once more Christian Churchmen, to you I appeal,
As to high-minded men, who have hearts that can feel;
Place a Chest in the Church for the silver and gold,
(There's a box for the National Schools I am told)
Shake yourselves from the dust of a contest so mean,
And without any Rate keep the Parish Church clean.

BIBLIOGRAPHY

GENERAL

Philipot, J. and T. *Villare Cantianum*, 1659.

Harris, J. *History of Kent*. London, 1719.

Seymour, C. *Survey of the County of Kent*. Canterbury, 1776.

Hasted, E. *History of the County of Kent*. Canterbury, 1798.

Ireland, W. H. *History of the County of Kent*. London, 1828.

Bagshaw, S. *History and Directory of the County of Kent*. Sheffield, 1847.

Jessup, F. W. *A History of Kent*. Finlayson, London, 1958.

Jessup, F. W. *Kent History Illustrated*. Kent County Council, 1966.

Burrows, M. *Cinque Ports*. Longmans Green, London, 1888.

Bucknall, R. *Boat Trains and Channel Packets*. London, 1957.

Nock, O. S. *The South Eastern and Chatham Railway*. Ian Allan, 1961.

Wallenberg, J. K. *Kentish Place Names. The Place Names of Kent*. Uppsala, 1931.

Ekwall, E. *Dictionary of Place Names*. Oxford, 1940.

LOCAL

Stock's Illustrated Handbook of Folkestone and its Neighbourhood. H. Stock, 1865.

English's Handbook of Folkestone for Visitors. S. J. Mackie. 9th Edition, 1874.

S. J. Mackie. *Folkestone and its Neighbourhood*, with *Gleanings from the Municipal Records*. 1883.

Woodward, M. *The Parish Church of Folkestone*. Skeffington & Son, London, 1892.

Winbolt, S. E. *Roman Folkestone*. Methuen, 1925.

Glanfield, W. G. *Rambles Around Folkestone*. Parsons, 1900.

Walton, J. G. (ed.). *Folkestone and the Country Around*. 1925.

Jones, L. R. *Metropole Folkestone, The Old . . . The New*. 1969.

Howarth, R. (ed.). *Folkestone, Past and Present*. 1954.

Neason, H. A. *Borough of Folkestone: The Town Council, Its Services and Administration*. 1968.

BIBLIOGRAPHY

INDEX